SHROPSHIRE HISTORY MAKERS

SHROPSHIRE
HISTORY MAKERS

Dorothy P.H. Wrenn

E P PUBLISHING LIMITED

This edition first published 1975 by EP Publishing Limited
East Ardsley, Wakefield, Yorkshire, England

ISBN 0 7158 1096 0

The author gratefully acknowledges the following
for kindly supplying photographs:

Local History Department, Shrewsbury Library
(Pages 7, 11, 13, 15, 24, 37, 38, 54, 60, 67);
National Portrait Gallery (9, 14, 29, 59); National
Maritime Museum (22); Radio Times Hulton Pic-
ture Library (16, 69); H. Griffiths (30, 46); Clive
House Museum (31, 52, 56); R. Carter (41);
Wellcome Institute (45, 49); Mrs. T. Ewart (57);
Oswestry Public Library (61); Royal College of
Surgeons (66); W. Bishop (73); Save The Children
Fund (74); Mr & Mrs Lionel Jebb (75, 78);
National Library of Wales (82); 'Oswestry Adver-
tiser' (88); Robert Jones and Agnes Hunt
Orthopaedic Hospital (89, 95).

Please address all enquiries to EP Publishing Limited
(address as above)

Text set in 11/12 pt. Photon Baskerville, printed by photolithography,
and bound in Great Britain at The Pitman Press, Bath

Preface

In a book of this size, it is impossible to make a comprehensive selection of figures important in the history of a county; some have to be omitted. I have tried to include a variety of period and of talent, and while some obvious personalities appear, others who are less well-known, but, I hope, of equal interest, have also been included.

So many people have helped me with information and pictures that it is impossible to mention every one. I would like, however, to put on record my debt to the Staff of various Shropshire Libraries, in particular Miss H. Williams, of the Local History Department at Shrewsbury, and Mr W. Walpole, of Oswestry, who have so kindly put at my disposal a great deal of information and illustrative material.

My thanks are also due to Mr Cruttenden, of the Robert Jones and Agnes Hunt Hospital, Gobowen; to Captain Hunt, of Boreatton Hall, Baschurch; to Mr and Mrs Lionel Jebb, Ellesmere; to the Save The Children Fund, and to Mr J. Wilson of Guildford, all of whom were good enough to give me access to personal or family records.

I am also indebted to Mr R. James, of Clive House Museum, who supplied me with a photograph of a previously unpublished portrait of Telford as a young man, and to Mr Cross, of Shrewsbury, for his careful reproduction of prints and pictures, many of which reached him in a very faded condition.

The photograph of Sir Walford Davies is taken from one in the possession of the National Library of Wales, Aberystwyth. As all my enquiries as to the identity of the photographer have been without result, I hope that this will be accepted as sufficient acknowledgement of its use. I was especially anxious to include it because it is the most sympathetic likeness I have seen of the subject.

Dorothy P. H. Wrenn

Contents

John Talbot, Earl of Shrewsbury c. 1390–1453

John Talbot, Earl of Shrewsbury.

The period of the Hundred Years War between England and France is so distant that, in many aspects, it is difficult to infuse it with any sense of reality. It has become a jumble of dates and battles, of place names which are vaguely familiar because they are connected with the campaigns of 1914–1918 and 1939–1944. The characters involved in the long drama are, in general, shadowy figures, half mythological, difficult to visualise as men and women of flesh and blood, whose emotions and ambitions resembled our own. Occasionally, glimpsed in the dusty pages of ancient documents, some of them spring to life: Edward III was one, John of Gaunt another; and, in the second half of the War, between the glamour of Henry V and the mysticism of Joan of Arc, John Talbot of Whitchurch, Earl of Shrewsbury, emerges as a personality in his own right; quick-tempered, ambitious, imperfect, human and brave.

He was born in or about 1390. His father, Richard Talbot of Goodrich, in Herefordshire, had inherited the estates of several heiresses. (Although the original Talbots were not of aristocratic lineage, they had for generations improved their standing by marriages with only daughters of noblemen.) In keeping with the family tradition, this Richard Talbot married Ankaret, daughter and sole heiress of John Le Strange of Blakemere, near Whitchurch. The prefix 'Blake' comes from the Saxon 'blaecan' meaning bleached, so Blakemere meant 'White Mere', or, later, the Mere by the White Church (Whitchurch). On the south side of the lake, a mound marks the site of the Le

7

Strange Manor House, which was still standing in the early years of the 17th Century, but has long since disappeared. Richard Talbot attended several of Edward III's Parliaments as Lord Talbot of Blakemere, so he probably spent a great deal of time at his wife's home, where his children were born.

John Talbot was the second son of the marriage. He had an elder brother, Gilbert, and at least two younger ones—probably more. In 1404 he was married to Maud Neville, in whose right he held the baronies of Furnivall and Hallamshire. The possessions of an heiress invariably came to her husband, since a woman was incapable of bearing arms.

Childhood did not last for long in the fifteenth century. John, married at 14, was taking an active part in battle before he was 17 years of age. Times were unsettled on the Welsh Border. Henry IV had deposed Richard II and taken the crown, but his hold on the kingdom was a precarious one. In 1403 he had put down a rebellion, instigated by the Welshman Owain Glyn Dwr and led by the Percy brothers, Earls of Northumberland and Worcester, at the Battle of Shrewsbury. The Percys were subdued, but Owain Glyn Dwr continued to urge his compatriots to abrogate English rule. In 1406, John Talbot was knighted after serving in Wales under Edward Charlton, Lord Powys. In 1407, he became Constable of Montgomery Castle and in the same year took part in the siege of Aberystwyth, which fell to an English Army led by Prince Henry, later Henry V. The following year he, and his elder brother, Gilbert, laid siege to Harlech Castle, which held out until 1409. When the castle was finally taken, some of Glyn Dwr's family were among the prisoners. But Owain himself escaped, and continued to incite rebellion in Wales until 1413, when he disappeared, presumably dying at about that time.

From the capture of Harlech Castle until the death of Henry IV in 1413, Sir John Talbot's fortunes are obscure, but the first months of the new reign found him a prisoner in the Tower of London. That Henry V should have so treated his successful commander, the Lord of large estates on the Welsh border, a man obviously faithful to the House of Lancaster, is strange. The two must have met during the course of the Welsh Wars; both fighting men, and must have admired each other's prowess. Henry could have had no reason for jealousy of a subject. The most likely explanation seems to be that Talbot was suspected of heresy. He may not have been involved with the Lollards himself, but his friends, and some of his relations most certainly were.

The Lollards, followers of John Wycliffe, had been a proscribed sect since 1406, but on the whole they had been left in peace. Henry IV was no bigot, and his father, John of Gaunt, had given Wycliffe protection. The Lollards demanded that the Bible be read aloud in English in churches. They denied the doctrine of transubstantiation, and felt that confession to a Priest was superfluous since God alone could pardon sin. Many scholars, clerics and well-known men had leanings towards Lollardism, one of the most prominent being Sir John Oldcastle, a famous military commander and a friend of both the young King and the Talbot family. When Henry V came to the throne, the orthodox clerics accused Oldcastle, who was imprisoned in the Tower. Imprisoned with him was Sir Thomas Talbot, of Faversham in Kent.

Oldcastle later escaped and was protected by the Abbot of Shrewsbury and the Prior of Wenlock, eventually returning unharmed to his native Herefordshire. Both Shropshire and the Talbot family were implicated in his escape from ecclesiastical justice. Sir John Talbot, his comrade-in-arms, was a Shropshire man, and it is a reasonable assumption that he was sent to the Tower on suspicion of conspiracy with the heretics. He was not kept there for very long, however; as early in 1414 he was released and sent to Ireland as Lord Lieutenant, for a term of six years. Was King Henry carefully removing a fellow-soldier from a potentially dangerous position?

In the 15th Century, Irish affairs appear to have been as confused and as turbulent as they are in the 20th. It is true that there were no schismatic complications, but land tenure, tradition, settlements and a complete lack of mutual trust make the record of Irish problems in documents 400 years old very little different from the same subject in today's newspapers. The Irish had never come under the influence of the Roman Empire and, cut off from England by the Irish Sea, they were even less prone than the Welsh or the Scots to absorb any vestige of European culture. The Norman Kings had made some attempt at conquest; powerful barons like Strongbow and de Lacey held Irish land in fealty to Henry II and King John. But before long, the Anglo-Norman landlords began to quarrel over their territorial rights. There were marriages with Irish heiresses which further complicated the issue. Irish 'Kings' (chieftains), like the Fitzgeralds and the Desmonds, held firmly to their own domains. There were frequent battles between Irish and English lords over land tenure, while both were prepared to resist any interference from the Crown unless it suited their interests. The post of the King's Lieutenant in Ireland was not an enviable one.

Sir John Talbot held this difficult office three times, in 1414, in 1424 and again in 1445. Only once, however, between 1414 and 1420, did he complete the full six years of his appointment.

He arrived in Ireland for the first time on 9th November, 1414, to find the South in a state of anarchy. A week later he decreed that no gold or silver should be taken out of the country without his express permission. In February, 1415, he besieged the castle of the

Irish chieftain, O'More of Leix. He captured the castle after a few weeks, freed O'More's English prisoners and took his young son as a hostage, to be brought up amongst the English. O'More made peace soon afterwards, promising to help Talbot to subdue other Irish leaders.

Realising the difficulty of the terrain, Talbot ordered a clear road to be cut through the forest of Armagh, along which he could move his army quickly in order to attack other Irish Chiefs, in particular O'Hanlon and O'Nele, whose prestige in arms was great. By the end of 1415 he had secured the co-operation of the greatest of the Irish lords, and could turn his attention to the land-grabbing ambitions of the Anglo-Irish settlers.

This was a more difficult matter. So long as he concentrated upon subduing the Irish, the English landowners were prepared to support him; when he began to investigate their own doings he met with hostility and a complete lack of co-operation. Talbot realised that his only chance of maintaining the uneasy peace in Ireland lay in his army, now augmented by the followers of his new Irish allies. But soldiers have to be paid, and money was not forthcoming. He had been promised 4,000 marks a year to pay his men. It was not sent and desertions began. In April, 1416, Talbot was in England, asking for the payment of his soldiers and of his own salary, and urging that more English settlers be sent out to Ireland. But the council was in no mood to listen to his demands. In 1415, Henry V had won the Battle of Agincourt. He and all his advisers were concerned with following up the victory in France, and Ireland was of no account. Instead of his 4,000 marks, Talbot was granted 400, which did little to alleviate the demands of his army.

Meanwhile, the Irish commoners had sent a petition to the King, in which they alleged that they were being grossly misused, by both the Anglo-Irish and the Barons of

Irish descent. Their leaders were being held without trial, the Irish chieftains oppressed them and the English landlords took their cattle and grain. Moreover, the unfortunate Lieutenant was held responsible by all parties, "carrying along with him the curses of many, because he, being runne much in debt for victuals, and divers other things, would pay little or nothing at all." Obviously, neither the Irish nor the Anglo-Irish could see Talbot's point of view; if the Crown would not grant him money to pay his men, he must let them re-imburse themselves in some way or else they would desert. If the army deserted, how could the King's rule in Ireland be maintained?

When he returned to Ireland early in 1417, Talbot acted decisively and with impartiality, insisting that both the Irish chiefs and the Anglo-Irish landlords treated their tenants with more justice. The Irish appear to have held him in respect and some affection after this, for when next he proposed to return to England, sometime in 1418, they petitioned him not to go.

During his first term as Lieutenant a quarrel began between Sir John Talbot and the Earl of Ormonde, an Anglo-Irish landowner, which was destined to dominate Irish politics for the next thirty years. Its cause is obscure—probably personal incompatibility. It is quite likely that Talbot, struggling with the complications of Irish politics, envied Ormonde and his brother their freedom to win glory in the French wars. In 1419, at the siege of Rouen, the Ormondes led "eighteen score men with red shields and eighteen score with pure white shields; and not often has so numerous and well-born a host embarked from England." But, at that same siege, Talbot's elder brother, Gilbert, was killed.

So in 1419 Talbot, already fully occupied in Ireland, was left guardian of his niece Ankaret, aged 12, and all the Talbot and Le Strange lands in England. He was bitterly disliked by the Anglo-Irish, who despised him because he treated the Irish chieftains on terms of equality. In 1420, however, he was recalled to England. Ankaret had died, leaving him heir to all the Talbot estates. But his successor as Lieutenant in Ireland was his enemy Ormonde.

Henry V appears to have realised that in Sir John Talbot he had a servant of unusual integrity combined with military genius. There was nothing self-seeking about Talbot; his duty was to serve his King, and personal considerations took second place. The thing he prized above all was honour and reputation. He was a soldier, his profession was arms; in the age of chivalry he fought according to the rules. It is said that, in recognition of the fact that his sword was an extension of its owner's personality, he had engraved upon the blade: "Sum Talbot, pro vincere inimicos meos", and his enemies were any enemies of the King.

Henry V knew this well enough. His marriage with the French princess Catherine, the agreement made at Troyes that France was to be handed over to him and to his heirs, did not please the French. In 1421, there were revolts in the districts around Paris. Talbot, newly back from Ireland, was ordered to quell these. He demolished Melun, Laval and Montargis, and was made a Knight of the Garter as a reward.

In 1422, Henry V died, suddenly and unexpectedly, leaving an infant son, Henry VI, as heir to both kingdoms. His younger brother, the Duke of Bedford, became Regent. In 1424, the Duke ordered Talbot to return to Ireland, for a second term as Lieutenant-Governor. But Ormonde, deposed and jealous, fomented rebellion amongst the Irish, and in 1427 Bedford summoned Talbot to France, leaving the unenviable task of governing Ireland to the Earl of March.

In France, a peculiar situation had arisen, which was beyond Bedford's comprehension. Jeanne d'Arc, a farmer's daughter from Domrémy, had become the leader of a great resistance movement in favour of the Dauphin, the rightful heir. In some strange way, she compelled men to follow her—seasoned campaigners like La Hire and Poton de Xantrailles. Under her command, the French were winning battles. The thing was incredible—there was talk of witchcraft; certainly the English soldiers feared her. Bedford felt that Talbot, who in his period of service in Ireland had become inured to the uncanny, might deal with her.

From the first, Talbot appears to have taken Jeanne seriously. Knowing that she intended to capture Orleans, he gave orders that a series of strong points, well away from the city, should be fortified. One after another, they fell, until by the end of May, 1429, only two, Meury and Janville, remained in English hands. Talbot agreed with his fellow-commander, Sir John Fastolfe, to make a stand on rising ground near to the village of Patay, two miles away from Janville, hoping that, as at Agincourt, the English archers would destroy the French cavalry. But as soon as the French army came in sight Fastolfe and his soldiers fled, leaving Talbot, with only 6,000 men, to face the enemy. So rapid was the French attack that the archers had no time to prepare their bows for action. In the fierce hand-to-hand fighting that followed, Talbot was unhorsed. Then his personal bodyguard, all Whitchurch men, raised the cry of "A Talbot! To the rescue!" and surrounded him as he lay helpless on the ground, guarding their leader until every one of them was killed and Sir John was taken prisoner.

He remained in French hands until 1433. He played no part in the trial and execution of Jeanne d'Arc, but during his imprisonment he made his will. In it, he gave explicit orders that his heart was to be buried in the porch of the Parish Church of St. Alkmund at Whitchurch, "that as the men of

Whitchurch had strode over him and fought for him in life, so their descendants should stride over and guard his heart when dead."

Of course, the French demanded an impossible sum as ransom for so important a prisoner. He was the only captive whose release Parliament was prepared to obtain by a public subscription, and the Crown—in the person of Bedford—expressed an intention of contributing "right notably". But in 1433 Poton de Xantrailles was taken by the English, and the French, weakened in morale since Jeanne's execution, were ready to arrange an exchange. Bedford demanded Sir John Talbot.

On his return to England, Talbot learned of the death of his wife. He soon remarried, however. Margaret Beauchamp, daughter of the Earl of Warwick, was a young heiress. She became the mother of Talbot's youngest and best loved son, John, Lord Lisle.

Margaret Beauchamp, second wife of John Talbot.

In 1434, Talbot was back in France, fighting against Charles VII and in alliance with the Duke of Burgundy. He captured the town of Honfleur and drove the French from Pontoise. So great were his successes at this time that, so it was said, the rumour of his coming was sufficient to terrify the French, and in Lorraine and Picardy mothers used to silence their disobedient children with the threat "The Talbot is coming".

In 1442 he was sent to England for reinforcements and returned to France an Earl. Although he is always referred to as the Earl of Shrewsbury, his original title was "Earl of Salop", for he took it from the shire, not from the town.

In 1445, negotiations were completed for the marriage of young Henry VI to Margaret, the lovely daughter of King René of Anjou. The Earl of Shrewsbury and his wife had the honour of escorting the new Queen to England, and Talbot appears to have given her his complete allegiance. Years later, when the struggle between York and Lancaster had begun, it is said that the Earl, hearing a lady of the Court speak slightingly of the Queen, rebuked her angrily with the words "Madame, you have to thank God this day that you are a woman."

He presented to Queen Margaret an illuminated folio, still to be seen in the British Museum, which shows him in a new light, as a patron of the Arts. The title page depicts the young King and Queen seated while the Earl, kneeling, hands her the book. The throne stands under a blue canopy decorated with golden stars; the royal couple are robed in crimson and purple; the Earl has with him his dog—a "Talbot" or Greyhound. The title page and subsequent marginal decorations are of daisies (Marguerites), a delicate compliment to the Queen's name.

In 1445 Talbot was in Ireland once again, where his old quarrel with Ormonde flared up anew. On the surface, there was a reconciliation. Ormonde's daughter,

Elizabeth, was married to one of Talbot's sons, and Talbot was created Earl Waterford. He made a curious law, which would doubtless be as unpopular now as it was in 1446. Anyone who claimed to be of English descent should "wear a beard on the upper lip alone", and must shave at least once a fortnight! The Irish declared that "from the time of Herod there came not any so wicked in evil deeds."

Three years later he was recalled to France, where he was again taken prisoner. For nine months he was kept as a hostage at Dreux, and as one of the conditions of his release Charles VII obtained from the English the town of Falaise. He also insisted that the Earl made a pilgrimage to Rome, thus ensuring for several months the absence of "one whose name was . . . dreadful to the French nation and much renowned among all other people".

By the spring of 1453, the English hold on France was being slowly and insidiously eroded. But there some districts which preferred English rule. The citizens of Bordeaux sent an embassy to England stating that, if an English army were sent to Gascony, the whole province would rise in revolt and join them. Talbot was given the title of Lieutenant of Aquitaine and put in command of this hopeless enterprise.

He landed near Bordeaux, in a creek still known as "The English Landing-Place". At first he was successful and marched triumphantly through Gascony, leaving garrisons to hold towns and castles as he passed and in this way depleting his own forces. The French King, determined to resist this new English invasion, came to Bordeaux at the head of an army of 12,000 men, 7,000 of whom were deployed to besiege the Castle of Castillon, one of the English strongpoints. Talbot, accompanied by his son, Lord Lisle, left his main force and returned with 8,000 horsemen to relieve the castle.

Castillon stood at the head of a small

valley between the Dordogne river and its tributary, the Lidore. On the slopes which flanked its approaches the French had position cannon—"300 pieces of ordonnance". Talbot, with a fine contempt for these new weapons, ordered his men to attack on foot, interlocking their shields as protection, though he himself, as a concession to his advanced age, remained mounted, conspicuous by his crimson cloak and white charger. (He was 63, a very old man by medieval standards.)

The venture was a lost cause from the start. No sooner were the English within the confines of the valley than Breton foot-soldiers cut off their retreat. Then the French opened fire; Talbot's horse was killed by a cannon-ball, and his forces fled in confusion. Talbot was killed by the blow of a battle-axe while he lay on the ground. Other blows followed, so that his head was mangled almost beyond recognition. "So they killed him", wrote Holinshead, "Whome they durst never look in the face when he stood upon his feet". Lord Lisle, the son of his old age, is said to have refused his father's command to save himself, and died with him.

After the battle, the Heralds of both sides walked about the field to identify the bodies of the slain. The great Earl was recognised by his personal Herald—a Whitchurch man—"by the loss of his teeth". The Herald knelt down, kissed his master and exclaimed:

Oh, my lord, my master, is it you? I pray God to pardon you all your sins. I have been your Herald for above forty years, but now I must leave you.

He then divested himself of his surcoat, which bore the Talbot Arms, and with it covered the Earl's body.

After his death, the Earl's heart was taken to Whitchurch and buried in the Church porch, according to his wish. His body was buried in Rouen Cathedral, where it remained for about 75 years. Then, during the early years of Henry VIII's reign, his grandson, Sir Gilbert Talbot, had the skeleton exhumed and brought to Whitchurch, where it was placed in a stately tomb, surmounted by a magnificent monument.

It is interesting to note that in 1711, when the old Whitchurch church collapsed and the ground had to be cleared for rebuilding, both heart and skeleton were found, though the tomb was destroyed. The heart, enclosed in an urn which also contained Talbot's rosary in a crimson velvet purse, was re-buried inside the new church. The skeleton was also re-buried, in a stone sarcophagus. The result of the fatal blow which broke the skull was plain to see, and inside the skull—most pathetic of all—lay the skeleton of a mouse which had crept in through the hole and made herself a nest! So the great Talbot, "Earl of Shrewsbury, Earl of Waterford, Marshall of France, Lord Strange of Blakemere and many other lands beside" shared his last resting-place with a mouse! But during his life-time a chronicler described him as "The bravest and most vigorous English General of them all", while his French enemies in Guienne referred to him as "Le Roi Talbot".

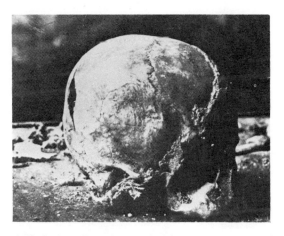

Skull of John Talbot, photographed during reconstruction of his tomb, and showing the fatal wounds received at Castillon.

13

Judge Jeffreys 1645–1689

George, first Baron Jeffreys of Wem.

For generations the name of Judge Jeffreys has evoked horror; even today, he is remembered by the average person as "Bloody Jeffreys", or "The Hanging Judge". At first glance, it appears that he should be listed as the most inglorious of Salopians. But was he so black as he was painted? He chose the wrong side in politics—a Royalist at a time when the restored Stuart monarchy remained balanced on a knife-edge. His character was further blackened by Macaulay, who, writing 160 years after his death, had not a good word to say for him. Perhaps now, he can be viewed in perspective. The 170 executions which followed the Bloody Assizes become insignificant when compared with the mass graves in the concentration camps of Hitler and Stalin. The men and women condemned by Jeffreys were executed according to the custom of the times—he did not invent the barbarous sentence of "hanging, drawing and quartering". As for Macaulay's accusations of sadism, ignorance of the law, and drunkenness, they are not substantiated by contemporary evidence. Jeffreys was a brilliant exponent of jurisprudence, eager to serve the Stuarts—one of whom, James II, simply used him as a tool, and then abandoned him. His portrait shows a sensitive face, and he appears to have been scholarly, tenacious in his affections and loyal to his friends. The opprobrium heaped upon him was largely the result of his unfailing support of the Stuart cause.

George Jeffreys was born on May 15th 1645, at Acton Park, near Wrexham, so that he was not a Salopian by birth. However, his father, John Jeffreys, held property in Shrewsbury. During the Civil War, John Jeffreys was a Royalist supporter, and, when Charles I visited Shrewsbury and granted the Borough a new Charter, in 1638, he became a member of the new Town Council. However, when the town was taken by the Parliament in 1645, John Jeffreys escaped to Acton, where he was in residence at the time of the birth of his son, George, on May 15th that year. He did not give up his property in Shrewsbury. In 1652, he was still a burgess of the town when his elder sons were entered as pupils at Shrewsbury School on 17th November. One of George's classmates was Wycherley, the dramatist, from whose father he bought land in his later, more affluent, years. He seems to have been a clever child. At fourteen, his father sent him as a boarder to St. Paul's School, London—Samuel Pepys' old school—and at sixteen he was removed to Westminster, probably because there he

would have a better chance of University entrance. George Jeffreys valued his education, and frequently referred to his schooldays in his later years.

Although he entered Trinity College, Cambridge, in 1662, a fellow student of Isaac Newton, it took him only a few months to discover that academic life was not his métier. In 1663, much against the wishes of his father, he was accepted as a member of the Honourable Society of the Inner Temple, having decided to become a barrister.

He was a student at the Inner Temple during the years of the Plague and Fire of London, studied assiduously, and although, like the majority of students, he was poor, his good looks and good manners made him popular wherever he went. During the Plague year, 1665, there was a dearth of lawyers because so many had either succumbed or fled from the City. Jeffreys took advantage of the situation to appear at Kingston Assizes, where he obtained briefs as though he were a

The Old School, Shrewsbury.

fully-fledged barrister; he pleaded with brilliance and remained undetected, though he had not yet completed his statutory five years as a student. He was living on a very small allowance from his father, but he loved the good things of life—books, food, drink and fine clothes—and, as his income was insufficient to provide all these, he decided to marry an heiress.

He began to pay court to the daughter of a wealthy country gentleman at whose house he was a frequent visitor. The young lady was impressed, but she was given little opportunity to see George alone. She had a companion, however, a clergyman's daughter named Sarah Neesham, who readily acted as go-between. Since there was little likelihood of obtaining her father's consent to the marriage, the lady agreed to elope with George, and arrangements were made accordingly. But at this point the father intercepted their correspondence, locked his daughter in her room, and dismissed her companion, who took refuge with a friend in Holborn.

The first intimation George Jeffreys had of the disaster came in a tear-blotted note from Sarah. He went to Holborn, talked to her, and suddenly became aware of two important facts—she was much prettier than her wealthy mistress and she had ruined her prospects of future employment for his sake. On the spur of the moment, he proposed marriage to her, and was accepted. The wedding took place on May 23rd, 1667, and for eleven years they lived in complete happiness. Her death left him desolate, and though he married a second time he never forgot his youthful love for Sarah. Years later, when he himself was dying, having touched the pinnacles of success and the depths of degradation, his last request was to be buried "as near as may be to my former wife, Sarah".

In 1668, George Jeffreys was called to the Bar. He rented a set of chambers in Kings Bench Walk, and waited for briefs.

At that period, Law and Politics were intermingled in a way which now seems incredible. A barrister's success depended upon his friends, and his friends depended upon their political success. Politics were not considered a matter for the general public. True, two parties were beginning to emerge, the Whigs and the Tories. The Whigs tended to hark back to the days of the Commonwealth; they were mainly wealthy Nonconformists, supporting the restored Monarchy largely in their own interest and because of Charles II's tact and discretion. But they hated Catholicism, as Samuel Pepys had already found to his cost during his period of service at the Admiralty under the Catholic James, Duke of York, the King's brother. The Tories, on the other hand, were High Anglican or Catholic in their views, looked back at the Protectorate with horror, and were ready to support the Stuarts in all things. There were elections of a kind, but manhood suffrage was undreamed of. The real power lay with the King, the nobility, and the City of London.

George Jeffreys, brought up in a Royalist household, was innately Tory in his outlook. Briefs, however, were to be sought in the City of London, and the City Corporation was fundamentally Whig. He frequented the City courts and was soon noticed, at first for his loud, booming voice, later for his brilliant exposition of points of law. The combination of these qualities came near to bringing the young barrister's career to an ignominious close, for Jeffreys soon became involved in what would now be termed a demonstration against the Lord Mayor of London.

One result of this escapade was that it brought Jeffreys to the notice of various Tory Aldermen who disliked the Lord Mayor. One of them, whose name was also Jeffreys, though no relation, took his young namesake under his protection and furthered George's interests, so that in 1671, at the age of 25, he became Common Serjeant of the City of London.

This office made him one of the two judges permanently in session at the Old Bailey, but he was free to carry on his practice in other courts when time allowed. It also brought him a house in Aldermanbury and the right to attend meetings of the Corporation of the City of London, and this led to one of his few acts of disloyalty. He was introduced to Chiffinch, Charles II's "page"—his office was really that of a confidential secretary. Chiffinch intimated that His Majesty would be grateful for information about the meetings of the Corporation, and Jeffreys, at heart a Royalist, agreed to give it. It may be argued that he was betraying a position of trust; on the other hand, he never swerved in his loyalty to the Stuarts, whom he served faithfully until his death. He would have argued that service to the King took precedence over service to the City. His action brought him in touch with the Royal entourage. In 1677 Charles conferred a knighthood on him, and at the same time Sir George Jeffreys exchanged his stuff gown for a silk one, and became a King's Counsel, and a Bencher of the Inner Temple. The young man's success was assured.

The year 1678, however, brought him the greatest grief of his life, for his wife, Sarah, died, leaving him with two young children, Margaret and John. George mourned her sincerely; it is probable that she was the only person whom he ever truly loved. After Sarah's death his character hardened. He developed an indifference to the opinions of others, which from that time became obvious in both his public and private life. As though he could no longer bear to live permanently in the house in Aldermanbury, he bought a country estate in Buckinghamshire, and spent lavishly on furnishings for it. That summer, the King visited him, and "drank his health seven times". (It was at this time that Jeffreys hiself began to earn a reputation for heavy drinking, which he did not altogether deserve.) Before the end of the year, thanks to Charles' favour, Jeffreys was elected Recorder of London.

The Recorder did not act as a Judge in major trials. He attended the Lord Chief Justice, and his major duty was to pronounce the sentence of the court after the verdict had been given. Macaulay accuses him of taking a sadistic pleasure in doing this, emphasising the sentences by cruel and violent homilies during which he bawled at the condemned criminals like a madman. But it must be remembered that Jeffreys lived in a barbarous age; the sentences for various crimes were well-known in advance of pronouncement. His loud voice was an asset in his profession. A court of law in Stuart times was a noisier place than would be tolerated by any modern judge.

Jeffreys' comments did not lack humour. On one occasion he had to pass sentence on two brothers convicted of stealing lead from the roof of Stepney Church. Announcing a fine of twenty pounds apiece, he observed:

I find you are not churchmen in the right way, yet your zeal for religion is so great as to carry you to the top of the church. If this be your way of going to church, it is fit you should be taken notice of.

The following year was a busy one for Jeffreys, for it was the year of the notorious Popish Plot. Titus Oates, an individual of somewhat unsavoury reputation, claimed to have discovered a plot to murder the King and replace him by his Catholic brother, James, Duke of York. Charles did not believe Oates, but the Whigs in the Government, led by the Earl of Shaftesbury, were terrified at the prospect of a Catholic monarchy and acted upon Oates' information. Several innocent people, both prominent and humble, were arraigned for treason at the Old Bailey and sentenced to death, imprisonment, flogging or transportation. Anti-Catholic feeling ran high, and anyone connected with the Duke's household was in danger. Samuel Pepys, who had served him so well at the Admiralty Office, was at one time suspect. It must be stressed that Jeffreys did not try any of Oates' victims; that was the work of the Lord Chief Justice. The Recorder merely pronounced sentence, and the usual sentence for treason was to be hanged and publicly disembowelled. Privately, Jeffreys distrusted Titus Oates, but he did not let this interfere with his public duty.

Before the end of the year, James, Duke of York, fled to Holland. Probably on the advice of King Charles, he appointed Jeffreys to act as his Solicitor-General, or private legal secretary, during his absence. Jeffreys' acceptance of this post added to his unpopularity in the City, where he was already disliked. The Whig Aldermen had good reason to distrust him, and many of the citizens blamed him, unjustly, for the sickening holocaust which followed the Popish Plot. Rumours spread of his passionate temper and bouts of drinking; the truth was, he was already suffering from stone in the bladder, an agonising complaint which eventually caused his death, and he drank to relieve his pain. He never came into Court drunk, as his unfailing vigilance clearly demonstrates.

The following summer, Jeffreys remarried. His beloved Sarah had been dead for more than a year and this time his head ruled his heart, for he married for money. The bride, Lady Ann Jones, was a young widow, daughter of one of the richest men in London, Sir Thomas Bludworth. Sir Thomas, who had been Lord Mayor of London at the time of the Great Fire, was Member of Parliament for the Borough of Southwark. He approved of his daughter's marriage to the handsome Recorder, which took place at the Church of St. Mary the Virgin, Aldermanbury.

The new Lady Jeffreys was not yet twenty, but she possessed a sharp tongue, and

though he remained faithful to her, Jeffreys' second marriage was not so happy as his first.

Soon after his marriage, Jeffreys became a member of the Serjeants' Inn; he was also appointed Chief Justice of Chester. These favours, together with his natural arrogance, and obvious Tory leanings, added to his growing unpopularity. The Liverymen of the City, together with the Commons, determined to remove him from the office of Recorder. They communicated this decision to the King, who concurred, though with obvious reluctance, for he had found in Jeffreys a good servant. But in 1681 the political climate changed. Charles dissolved the Whig Parliament, and for the rest of his reign he ruled without one. Jeffreys again appeared in the London courts, this time as Crown Counsel.

In June, 1683, another plot against the King's life was disclosed, this time a genuine one, which came to be known as the Rye House Plot. The Lords Russell and Essex, Colonel Algernon Sidney and others plotted to assassinate both the King and the Duke of York, and to make Charles' illegitimate son, the Protestant Duke of Monmouth, King. Jeffreys led the prosecution for the Crown and the plotters were duly found guilty and executed, with the exception of the Earl of Essex, who committed suicide while in the Tower of London. Again, Jeffreys had been accused of callousness in the matter of Earl Russell's execution, but in proving the Earl's guilt he was only serving the King. Blame for the clumsiness of the Executioner, Jack Ketch, who took three strokes of the axe to behead Russell, cannot be ascribed to Serjeant Jeffreys.

In the Autumn of that year, Charles rewarded Jeffreys for his services by appointing him Lord Chief Justice. He was thirty-eight at the time, the youngest man ever to have held the office. He also became a member of the Cabinet, largely owing to the influence of the Duke of York, who saw in him a useful ally. For Charles' health was failing and though the Rye House plotters were dead, Monmouth was still alive; and Protestant Members of Parliament were trying to move an Exclusion Bill with the object of passing over the Catholic Duke and making Monmouth the King's successor. To his credit, Charles constantly refused to consider this; Monmouth was his favourite son, but he had no intention of allowing him to supplant James, his legitimate heir.

Charles II died in February, 1685, after a short illness following a stroke, and James II succeeded him. An avowed Catholic, lacking his brother's tact and commonsense, the new King's throne was insecure from the start. He had, however, the wisdom to keep with him such servants of the Crown as he knew would never be persuaded to throw in their lot with the illegitimate Monmouth. One of the first to receive a mark of Royal confidence was the Lord Chief Justice, whom the new King created a peer of the Realm.

Jeffreys must have guessed what was afoot, for early in the year, while Charles lay dying, he opened negotiations with his old schoolfellow, Wycherley, for the purpose of buying property in Shropshire. His father's Shrewsbury houses would naturally have passed to his elder brother, but the Jeffreys had family roots in the county, and from Wycherley George purchased the manors of Wem and Loppington, at a price of £9,000. He assumed the title of Baron Jeffreys of Wem, and designated Lowe Hall, about one-and-a-quarter miles from the town, as his residence in the area.

One of the first people against whom proceedings were taken in the new reign was Titus Oates, who was brought before the Lord Chief Justice and accused of perjury and slander. Jeffreys certainly enjoyed this trial, for he was convinced that, in addition to bringing about the deaths of several innocent victims, Oates had contributed to his own personal unpopularity, since he had been obliged to pronounce sentence upon them.

"You are a shame to mankind," he told the prisoner, before sentencing him to a heavy fine, a flogging, the pillory and a long term of imprisonment. Perjury was not a capital offence, and after the Revolution of 1688 the despicable Oates was set free—surely a more evil character than the Lord Chief Justice.

Another prisoner who appeared before Jeffreys at this time was Richard Baxter, the celebrated Nonconformist preacher. Baxter was a fellow Salopian, but Jeffreys took a great dislike to the old man, probably because he showed no fear of him, and stoutly denied the charge of seditious libel brought against him.

"Thou art one of the greatest rascals in the Kingdom," Jeffreys told him, and would obviously have liked to sentence him, also, to the pillory. But Baxter had influential friends, and got off with a fine of 500 marks.

That same year came Monmouth's Rebellion in the West Country, followed by his defeat and execution and the infamous circuit known as the "Bloody Assizes", when Jeffreys and four other judges toured Devon, Cornwall and Somerset to try the captured rebels. These trials have stained Jeffreys' name for the greater part of three hundred years, and a great deal that has been written about them gives him less than strict justice. A Royalist to the core, he certainly abhorred the rebellion, but, as has been pointed out before, his task was to administer the law; the penalties involved were already enacted by statute. In many cases, too, where the condemned were ignorant men swayed by Monmouth's dazzling promises and not fully understanding the implication of taking up arms against the King, he pronounced the more merciful sentence of transportation. Of 1,381 persons whom he sentenced, fewer than 200 suffered the death penalty.

When he returned to London, Jeffreys found James embittered by the Rebellion and determined to keep about him the few men

Judge Jeffreys bullying Richard Baxter.

whom he could trust. One of these was Jeffreys, who was made Lord Chancellor of England, with the duties of presiding over the House of Lords and keeping the Great Seal, without which no Bill could become law. The honour did not give Jeffreys unmitigated pleasure, for it kept him out of the courts, where his career had always lain. His private life, too, was far from happy at the time; he suffered constant pain from the stone, several of his children had died young, and his heir, the son of Sarah, was unreliable and wild. Added to this, his second wife, Ann, was constantly trying to promote the welfare of her own children and does not seem to have treated Sarah's as kindly as she might.

Jeffreys, though loyal to the Stuarts, was anti-Catholic, and refused to put his signature to the Declaration of Indulgence permitting freedom of worship for all sects, which James ordered to be read in churches throughout the Kingdom. As Lord Lieutenant of Shropshire he was obliged to investigate the feeling about the measure in his county, but he did not go in person, confining himself to writing to the Member for Shrewsbury instead.

The immediate result of the Declaration was that the Bishop of London and six other Bishops refused to have it read in their dioceses: they were arrested and imprisoned in the Tower, but in their trial and subsequent acquittal the Lord Chancellor had no part. He was, however, present as an official witness at the birth of James' son, which happened at the same time. The combination of these two events, the birth of a Catholic heir and the trial of seven leading churchmen, led directly to the Revolution of 1688 and the accession of William of Orange.

James, having secured the escape of his wife and child, took refuge in Whitehall and insisted on his Chancellor accompanying him, bearing the Great Seal, which he determined should not fall into William's hands. On the night of November 17th, however, James fled to France, one of his last acts being to take the Great Seal, which he threw into the Thames. (It was later dredged up by a fisherman.)

Jeffreys, finding himself abandoned by his master, also tried to escape. He arranged for a ship to carry him to France and then, disguised as a coal-heaver, went for a meal to an inn in Wapping known as the Red Cow. But a search party was already looking for him, and one of its members recognised him in spite of his blackened face. It was a scrivener, Burnham, who had said that he would never forget his face.

Jeffreys was hustled into a coach and driven through a hostile mob to the house of the Lord Mayor. The Londoners were ready to lynch him, but the Lord Mayor pitied him.

He gave him a meal and had him conveyed to the Tower, for his own safety.

And there he remained for four months. William of Orange became king, but was at a loss to deal with the man who was still, officially, Lord Chancellor of England. He had committed no crime, yet he was the most hated man in the kingdom. So he was lodged in the Bloody Tower, in reasonable comfort, and his family and friends were allowed to visit him.

What would have become of Jeffreys had he lived is an interesting speculation. Fortunately for the new government, they were spared the problem of dealing with him. His old complaint, the stone, took a fatal turn. In January, 1689, the symptoms of kidney degeneration began to show themselves. He was in great pain, with a high fever, vomiting continually, and realised that he had not long to live. But he lingered, in a pathetic state, until mid-April, stoutly maintaining that all his life he had sought only to serve his King and the Church of England. He died on April 19th and his last thoughts were of his first wife, Sarah, of whom he spoke tenderly, begging that he might be buried beside her in the church of St. Mary, Aldermanbury, and eventually, this last wish was carried out.

Poor George Jeffreys; he was not quite the wicked monster history has made him out to be, and he certainly never lacked courage. Shropshire historians have always been ashamed of him, but as Baron of Wem he brought two distinctions to the County. At forty, he was the youngest Lord Chancellor of England, and he is also the only Lord Chancellor ever to have died a prisoner in the Tower.

Admiral Benbow 1653–1702

Admiral Benbow, by Kneller.

It was during the last year of the reign of Elizabeth I that William Benbow, the second son of a farmer from Prees Heath, came to Shrewsbury as the apprentice of a local tanner. Some years later he opened a tannery of his own, which stood somewhere in Mardol. It must have been a family business, for both his sons went into partnership with him and one of them, also named William, inherited it on his father's death. The tannery did well in William's hands and he became a wealthy man. Perhaps the Civil War helped him to make his money, for leather was in great demand for boots, saddles and other accoutrement. Prudently, William Benbow avoided taking sides in the conflict; he applied himself to his trade and in 1649 became a Burgess of the town. He rented land on Coton Hill, where he built a substantial house for himself. One section of it still remains.

William's younger brother, John, threw in his lot with the Parliamentarians and left Shrewsbury, which was a Royalist stronghold, shortly after the outbreak of war. He soon became a captain, and when the Parliamentarian forces captured Shrewsbury, his knowledge of the locality was of great advantage to them. They gained admission by the Water Gate under cover of darkness, arrested all the leading citizens and obtained the keys of the castle. It was John Benbow who guided them through the streets to the homes of the men whom they wished to secure, and the Royalists were locked in the castle dungeons before daylight.

The execution of the King, however, was

an act which John Benbow could not con-
done. He changed sides, and at the Battle of
Worcester was fighting for the cause of
Charles II. When the Royalists were defeated,
John Benbow was taken prisoner. He was
brought back to Shrewsbury, where he was
tried for treason and desertion, found guilty
and executed by a firing squad in 1651. Two
years later, when William Benbow's only son
was born, he was given the name John in
memory of his uncle.

There is no record of the second John
Benbow's childhood, but it is possible to
make some assumptions with reasonable cer-
tainty. As his father was a Burgess, it is
probable that he was educated at the Grammar School, where any son of a Burgess could
be entered at a nominal fee. He was the only
son, so he would be a familiar figure at the
tannery from an early age. He became his
father's apprentice, and since he did not embark upon his sea-faring career until he was
twenty-four—a very advanced age for enlist-
ment in the Navy—he would have plenty of
time to complete the full seven years of
training.

In Shrewsbury, there is an old tradition
that John Benbow ran away to sea, leaving
the key of Benbow House hanging on a
broken twig on one of the trees in the garden,
but this legend will not stand up to examination. In the first place, at twenty-four, he
would be out of his apprenticeship and his
own master, so he would not need to run
away. Secondly, his father seems to have had
no objection to his son's sea-faring life; there
was no break in their relationship and
William bequeathed to him Benbow House
and the major part of his property. It is interesting to speculate on why this young
tanner abandoned a lucrative business in an
inland town, for there is no record of any
other member of the Benbow family having
followed the sea. Probably he longed for
adventure, like the Uncle he had never seen.
Probably the Severn lured him. It was then a
navigable river on whose waters broad
barges, known as "trows", conveyed goods
to the port of Bristol from as far upstream as
Welshpool. He would have plenty of opportunities to talk to seamen, and could well
have made the journey to Bristol himself, in
charge of a cargo of hides. The decision to
break with the family tradition must have
been reached only after careful deliberation,
for he was well into manhood before he took
the final step. In 1677 he joined the Royal
Navy, and a year later became Master's Mate
on board the *Rupert*, with Captain Herbert in
command.

The *Rupert* was ordered to the
Mediterranean on patrol duty, with instructions to guard British merchantmen from the
notorious Sallee Rovers which infested the
Levant and the North African coast. These
were pirate ships, usually manned by
Moorish crews, which lurked in their secret
harbours on the rocky Dalmatian Coast and
among the Greek islands, making of
themselves a perpetual hazard to ships
trading in the Mediterranean Sea. Benbow,
who appears to have possessed a cool, un-
imaginative kind of courage, so distinguished himself during the *Rupert*'s first
encounter with a pirate ship that he was
promoted from Master's Mate to Master and
transferred to the *Nonsuch*. As Master of the
Nonsuch, he served under Captain Rooke and
Captain Shovel. Both these gentlemen sub-
sequently rose to the rank of Admiral; they
spoke well of Benbow in later years and
furthered his promotion.

One of Benbow's traits of character was
his tactlessness, and this bade fair to ruin his
career at its outset. In 1681, still in the
Mediterranean, he was involved in another
brush with pirates. The *Adventure*, commanded by Captain Booth, attacked the
enemy first, but was beaten off. In response to
signals for help, the *Nonsuch* came to the
rescue, captured one of the pirate ships and
drove the others to seek shelter. There was

Benbow House, Shrewsbury (now demolished).

great triumph on board the *Nonsuch* and several derogatory comments were made on the seamanship of Captain Booth and the cowardly behaviour of his crew. When the flotilla was in port shortly after the action, Benbow repeated some of these remarks. His words came to the ears of Captain Booth, who was already smarting from his defeat, and as a result Benbow was arrested and brought before a court martial on board the flagship, the *Bristol*. It was obvious that he had been made the scapegoat, for several others were equally to blame and it was impossible to trace the originators of the ribald criticisms. However, he was found guilty of "repeating words humiliating to a senior officer", and sentenced to forfeit three months' pay, help tend the wounded men on board the *Adventure* and to make a public apology to Captain Booth before all the

officers of the squadron, who were assembled on the deck of the *Bristol* in order to hear him. The whole affair appears trivial enough, but, considering the severity of naval discipline at that time, he got off lightly.

In November of the same year the *Nonsuch* was ordered back to Spithead, where her entire company was paid off and disbanded. Benbow, probably in a disgruntled mood, did not look for another berth in the Royal Navy. Instead, he joined the crew of a merchantman engaged in trade between London, Bristol, Italy and Spain. His upbringing as a merchant's heir stood him in good stead, so that by the time he was thirty he was Captain and part-owner of the frigate *Benbow* and had amassed a considerable personal fortune. Had it not been for the Sallee Rovers, he would in all probability have spent the rest of his sea-faring days in a trading ship.

In 1686, however, while off the Balearic Islands, the *Benbow* was attacked and boarded by a Moorish raider from Algiers. Captain Benbow rallied his crew and fought so fiercely that the boarding party withdrew in great haste. Behind them on the *Benbow*'s deck they left the bodies of thirteen pirates, and before having them thrown overboard Benbow ordered them to be decapitated and their heads to be preserved in a tub of brine.

Captain Benbow's next port of call was Cadiz, where he had had numerous altercations with the Spanish Revenue officials on the subject of duties payable on the goods he carried. He decided to play a somewhat ghoulish practical joke on them. When the *Benbow* docked at Cadiz the captain went ashore, followed by his negro servant, who was carrying a leather sack, the neck of which was very firmly secured. The officials waiting on the wharf immediately demanded to know what the bag contained.

"Salt provisions, for my own use," was Benbow's reply.

The Revenue officers requested to inspect the contents of the bag, whereupon Benbow pretended to be very angry that they should suspect him of smuggling and refused to open it. The argument continued for a while, ending in Benbow's being escorted to the Custom House, where the local magistrates were sitting. They received him with great courtesy, but insisted that he opened the sack. Benbow then remarked, "I have told you that it contains salt provisions for my own use. Caesar, throw them down on the table, and, gentlemen, if you like them, they are at your service."

The boy unfastened the sack, and the thirteen heads rolled out onto the magistrates' table. Benbow then related the story of his fight with the pirates and the Spaniards were delighted to hear of the slaughter of the Algerians, who were a constant menace to shipping from Cadiz. They sent an account of the adventure to the King of Spain, who was so impressed that he wished to hear it from the English captain in person. So Benbow travelled to Madrid, where the King listened to his tale with approval and gave him a sum of money as a reward for his services. He was, however, unable to understand why a man who possessed such obvious gifts of leadership was commanding a mere merchantman. He related the story of Benbow's exploit in a letter to William III, who had just become King of England. As a result of his intervention Benbow rejoined the Navy in June, 1689, with the rank of Captain.

Benbow's next appointment was to the post of Master Attendant of Deptford Dockyard, a position which he held for the next six years. He was married by now, and rented Sayes Court, a house at Deptford belonging to the diarist, John Evelyn, for his wife and family. At this time the young Czar of Russia, Peter—later to become Peter the Great—was in Deptford with some of his entourage, studying British naval organisation and learning ship-building with a view to creating a Russian navy. Benbow was for a time responsible for the welfare of the Russian party, and when he was asked to find a house for them he sub-let Sayes Court, with Evelyn's consent. The Russians, however, were unaccustomed to the refinements of Western civilisation. They made havoc among curtains, books and furniture, and dug up the lawns and flower beds in order to construct for themselves what can only be described as an assault course over which they could leap and scramble. When Peter left England, both Benbow and Evelyn demanded that the Government should make good the damage done by their distinguished visitors. Benbow, supporting Evelyn, stated to the Treasury officials who were considering what sum to award in compensation: "The place was in so bad a condition that I can scarce describe it to your honours, besides much of the furniture broke, lost and destroyed". They were each awarded £350, a substantial sum. Sayes Court was presumably repaired and redecorated, for Benbow was soon back in residence, with a new tenancy agreement which specifically stated that he should "keepe the garden". Evelyn evidently had no intention of going to the expense of laying it out again.

Before long, Benbow was engaged on active service in the English Channel, keeping watch on French shipping in case of an attack on behalf of the exiled Stuarts, and protecting merchantmen—the equivalent of convoy duty. In 1693 he led an attack on the harbour of St. Malo, and a contemporary writer gives a full description of the event:

He arrived off the town on the 16th November, and anchoring within half a mile of it, cannonaded and bombarded it for three days successively. Then his men landed on an island, where they burned a convent. On the 19th they took the advantage of a dark night, a fresh gale and a strong tide to send in a fireship of a particular contrivance styled "The Infernal", in order to burn the town; but she struck upon a rock before she arrived at the place, and the engineer was obliged to set her on fire and retreat. She continued burning for some time, and at last blew up, with such an explosion as shook the whole town like an earthquake, unroofed three hundred houses, and broke all the glass and earthware for three leagues around. A Capstan, that weighed two hundred pounds, was transported into the place, and falling upon a house levelled it to the ground. The greater part of the wall towards the sea tumbled down and the inhabitants were overwhelmed with consternation, so that a small number of troops might have taken possession, but there was not a soldier on board. Nevertheless, the sailors took and demolished the Quince-fort, and did considerable damage to the town of St. Malo, which had been a nest of privateers that infested the English commerce.

In 1695 Benbow was in pursuit of the French Admiral, Du Bart, who was intercep-

ting English and Dutch merchant ships. The following year, under the command of his old captain, now Admiral Sir Cloudesley Shovell, he was wounded while taking part in the bombardment of Calais. His courage during this action was conspicuous—he was a man who was at his best under heavy fire—and he was rewarded by appointment to the rank of Rear-Admiral of the Blue. He spent the greater part of the next two years on active service in the Atlantic, protecting English shipping from attacks by French privateers.

He maintained his connection with his native town, inheriting the Coton Hill house on his father's death. What happened to the tannery is uncertain; it could well have been bought or managed by Robert Ridge, who married Benbow's youngest sister, Elizabeth, and whose descendants were living in the district up to the early years of the nineteenth century. Benbow's wife seems to have been a Shrewsbury girl, and there were probably family visits to Coton Hill, for he kept up a lifelong friendship with a neighbour, Nathaniel Baskerville, whom he named as one of the executors of his will. Benbow was certainly in Shrewsbury in June, 1698, when the Mayor, Robert Sheppard, gave a banquet in his honour and the Corporation paid for sack, sherry and claret for the feast.

In November of the same year he was ordered to the West Indies, with instructions to observe the Spanish settlements there and gather what information he could about the strength of Spanish shipping in the area. The West Indies provided invaluable bases for the Spaniards, the French and the English, and Benbow's main task was to demonstrate the supremacy of English sea power. He was also ordered to institute a hunt for pirates, who made their headquarters amongst the creeks of the smaller Caribbean islands. On his return to England he was promoted to the rank of Vice-Admiral in recognition of his services.

On the outbreak of war with France, it was obvious that a squadron of English ships would again have to be sent to the West Indies. Benbow's name was at once put forward as Commander. However, William III, wishing to protect him, offered the appointment at first to other officers. Unlike Benbow, these were amateur seamen, gentlemen of rank and wealth who had offered their services to the King without having any intention of risking their own necks. One after another, they declined.

"Then", the King is alleged to have said, "we must spare our beaux and send honest Benbow".

The Admiral was sent for, and King William informed him personally that, if he did not wish to accept the command, he was at liberty to refuse it.

"Sire," was Benbow's reply, "I do not think that I have the slightest claim to choose my battle-station. I am ready to go to the East or the West Indies, or wherever your Majesty considers my services to be necessary." Accordingly, he was appointed to command the West India squadron and in August, 1701, sailed from Spithead on board the flagship *Breda*, a man o' war of 70 guns.

Before setting sail for the West Indies, Admiral Benbow made his will. It was not a very lengthy document, but made his intentions plain. Dispensing with the usual platitudes, he briefly commended his soul to the protection of his Saviour, "hopeing . . . to receive a pardon for all my sinns. And my body I committ to the Earth or Sea as it shall please God to order, to be decently interred as my executors shall think meet." He then went on to dispose of his property. To his wife, Martha, he left an annual income of seventy pounds sterling, free of all tax, for the rest of her life, unless she remarried, in which case it was to cease immediately. The rest of his property, money and goods, was to be divided amongst his three sons and two daughters. He was more emphatic that his

children should share equally whatever was left, putting in a special clause to the effect that his heir should not claim more by right of being the eldest ". . . my will and intention being that he shall have no greater share or proportion than the rest". As executors he named his "loveing friends Thomas Waring of London, Merchant; Nathaniel Baskerville of Shrewsbury, Gentl. and Thomas Minshall of London, Fishmonger", to each of whom he left twenty pounds. Despite his successful career at sea, his roots remained in trade, and it was to two merchants and his old boyhood friend that he entrusted the administration of his estate.

The French, very sensible of the value of the West Indies to their trade routes, sent three squadrons to intercept the British ships, so Benbow prudently took shelter in the harbour of Port Royal, Jamaica. However, before long the French squadrons split up, leaving ten warships, commanded by Admiral du Casse, to police the waters between Jamaica, Cuba and Hispaniola. Benbow decided to attack them, and accordingly left Port Royal in Mid-August, 1702. He had seven ships, only one of which mounted 70 guns—four of the French were as heavily armed. But he expected Rear-Admiral Whitson to arrive with reinforcements, and did not want the enemy to escape.

He caught up with du Casse more quickly than he expected, however, and opened fire immediately. It was evening and Benbow determined to hold him until darkness fell. The next morning, he discovered that some of the Captains under his command, who were not so eager for battle as himself, had dropped back, well out of range of the French. Benbow, therefore, sailed the *Breda* into the centre of the enemy flotilla, ordering the other six ships to follow. Only two of them, the *Ruby* and the *Falmouth*, obeyed his signals, and of these the *Ruby* was soon so badly shattered that she was forced to put back to Port Royal. The *Breda* and the

Falmouth continued the battle, the Admiral constantly signalling to his Captains to return. They, however, continued to manoeuvre well out of range, doing no more than fire a broadside into one of the French ships which was already disabled and in retreat.

On the third day of the running battle one of Benbow's legs was shattered by chain shot. The injury was roughly dressed and splinted, and the Admiral insisted on having a hammock slung up on the quarter deck. In this he lay, and continued to direct the action.

In the midst of the battle one of his junior officers, coming up to him for orders, expressed his sorrow at the loss of his leg.

"I am sorry for it too," was the reply, "but I had rather have lost them both than have seen this dishonour brought upon the English nation. But, do you hear, if another shot should take me off, behave like brave men and fight it out."

By now the *Breda* was so badly damaged that she was obliged to retire in order to refit. During this interval, Benbow called his Captains to come aboard his ship for a council of war. He upraided them for their cowardice, but Kirkby, Captain of the *Defiance*, told him that he had better give up as, in view of the superior number of the French guns, there was no prospect of victory. Kirkby made it plain that he and his fellow-officers had no intention of recommencing the battle, so Benbow, who by now had been wounded in the face and arm as well as in the leg, reluctantly put back to Jamaica.

As soon as the *Breda* docked, a messenger came on board, carrying a letter for the Admiral. Its contents read as follows:

Sir,

I had little hopes on Monday but to have supped in your Cabin: it pleased God to order otherwise. I am thankful for it. As for those cowardly Captains who deserted you, hang them up, for by God they deserve it.

Du Casse

It was some time before Benbow could follow the advice of his admiring enemy, for his leg had to be amputated. He bore the pain stoically, and at first the wound appeared to be healing. Admiral Whitson arrived, and at the beginning of October he presided over a court martial, held on board the *Breda*, at which the surviving Captains, Kirkby, Wade, Constable, Vincent and Fogg, were arraigned for mutiny and for cowardice in the face of the enemy. Both Benbow and the Captain of the *Ruby* gave evidence, and Captain Vincent, who had been in command of the *Falmouth*, was immediately exonerated, for he had obeyed orders throughout the battle, retiring only when his ship was badly damaged. Kirkby and Wade were condemned to death and sent to England, where they were executed. Constable, who was stated to have been drunk throughout the entire engagement, was dishonourably discharged from the Navy and sentenced to a long term of imprisonment. Fogg was acquitted.

The exertion of being carried to the court martial and giving evidence re-opened Benbow's wound. Gangrene set in, he developed a high fever, and on 4th November, 1702, he died. He was buried at Kingston and his epitaph stated that he was "a true pattern of English courage, who lost his life in defence of his country".

His fellow citizens also remembered him. A monument was erected to his memory in St. Mary's, his parish church. Carved in relief on a white marble plaque, it shows his profile, and beneath it his ship, firing a broadside into an enemy vessel. The inscription describes him as "born at Coton Hill, in this Parish, and died at Kingston, Jamaica . . . of wounds received in his memorable action with the French Squadron, off Carthagena, in the West Indies, fought on the 19th and the five following days of August, in the year 1702".

Robert Clive 1725–1774

Robert Clive.

The fascination of Robert Clive lies less in the story of his brilliant and unorthodox career than in the irrelative elements of his character. Considered stupid, and with only a rudimentary education, he had the foresight to plan and carry out a campaign which won an empire. Possessed of a temper which blazed uncontrollably at the slightest hint of personal criticism, he displayed in battle a remarkable coolness and self-control. In spite of his boorish manners and love of ostentation, he won and kept the affection of a refined, cultured woman; their marriage was a relationship of perfect happiness which remained unbroken until his death. Outwardly hard and indomitable, he was inwardly so sensitive that loneliness and censure drove him to depression and, finally, despair. The behaviour of this strange man is indicative of an elemental psychopathic disorder.

Robert Clive was born on 29th September, 1725, at the Styche, his father's manor-house in the parish of Moreton Say, near Market Drayton. Richard Clive was a lawyer, not very well off, and Robert was his eldest son; the family grew to be a large one—five more sons and seven daughters.

From boyhood, Robert and his father were seldom in accord; temperamentally they were too much alike. When the boy was three years old, his mother, making the excuse that her other babies took up so much of her time that she was unable to give proper attention to her first-born, arranged for him to be fostered by an uncle and aunt in Manchester. This childless couple indulged

Clive House, Shrewsbury (Clive's town house while he was M.P. for Shrewsbury).

him in every way; until he was seven he ruled their household, totally uncorrected. He discovered quickly that the adult world would give in to temper tantrums, or try to coax him out of them with presents. When he returned home, after four years of spoiling, it is small wonder that his irascible father found in him "a fierceness and imperiousness that made him fly out at every trifling occasion". Belated attempts at discipline only aggravated the situation, until a breach opened between father and son which took over twenty years to heal.

Some of the madcap exploits of Robert Clive's boyhood have undoubtedly been exaggerated, though he was certainly expelled from three schools—Market Drayton, Merchant Taylors', and a private school at Hemel Hempstead. The notorious episode of his climbing the tower of Market Drayton Church was true, though not so daring as it first sounds, for he went up, quite safely, by the inner staircase used by the bell-ringers. Having reached the leads, he climbed over the coping and sat astride one

of the gargoyles, thoroughly enjoying the sensation he was causing among passers-by below. It is said that he carried out this piece of bravado in order to get out of the gargoyle's mouth a smooth pebble with which to play "ducks and drakes" on the river.

He also appears to have chosen undesirable companions, leading a gang of village lads who obtained bribes from the local shopkeepers by threatening to damage their property. Soon after, his father removed him from Market Drayton Grammar School to the Merchant Taylors' School: he hoped that the strict regime of a boarding school, combined with separation from his adoring mother, might curb Robert's wildness, but the hope was a vain one. The boy showed no aptitude for study, was repeatedly in trouble and was finally told to leave. One of the masters observed that, if he lived to grow up, which at times appeared an unlikely prospect because of his foolhardy ways, Clive would certainly make a name for himself. But this comment was no consolation to the disappointed father.

Market Drayton Church Tower.

It was May, 1744, when the *Winchester* anchored off Madras, and Clive's life in India began. The position of the East India Company at that time was an uneasy one. For almost two hundred years the British and French East India Companies had been establishing trading stations at various points on the Indian coast, their objective being peaceful commerce. At first, they had been protected by the Great Mogul, titular ruler of all India. But by 1744 the power of the Mogul was waning, the various local rulers, the Nawabs, were strong and hostile, and at each trading station a fort, housing a small army of white mercenaries and Indian sepoys, had been built as a protective measure. Each Company jealously watched the other's economic potential, for the War of the Austrian Succession was being waged in Europe, and despite the fact that their trading in India was ostensibly peaceful, the opportunity to seize an enemy station could be snatched by either side. The English had a fleet patrolling the coast off the French station at Pondicherry, while the French, under the Directorship of Joseph-Francois Dupleix, were engaged in intrigue with the local Nawab. But meanwhile, stalemate: in Madras and Pondicherry trade with the Indian merchants continued.

When Robert was seventeen, Richard Clive decided to wash his hands of this unsatisfactory son. He procured for him a post as a junior writer in the service of the British East India Company—salary £5 a year—and shipped him off to Madras.

Robert seemed to attract even the turbulence of the elements. His voyage lasted for fifteen months because his ship, the *Winchester*, was blown right off course and eventually ran aground off the coast of Brazil, where repairs had to be carried out. He fell overboard during this time and his rescue was the first of several incidents which led him to believe that he had a charmed life, and need not fear to face death.

Any life less suited to Robert Clive than that of a writer cannot be imagined. He, to whom action was vital, became a clerk. Day after day, perched on a stool in the "factory"—really a great warehouse which in no way resembled the modern interpretation of the word—he compiled lists of the goods brought in for shipping abroad. He was really an outsider and made no close friends among the other writers, his pay was meagre and he fell a victim to nervous depression, a condition then unrecognised as a mental illness but which was to recur more than once during his life.

First, he made himself unpopular by quarrelling with the official in charge of the underwriters, who demanded an apology. This Clive refused to give, but was compelled to do so by the Governor of the Madras factory. When he at last complied, the official who evidently wished the matter to be forgotten, invited him to dinner.

"No Sir," was Clive's reply, "The Governor commanded me to apologise, but he did not command me to dine with you."

Such an attitude did not make for popularity and the other young Englishmen left him to himself. One afternoon, while he was alone in the office, he tried to commit suicide, using a loaded pistol which he knew was kept in the drawer of one of the desks. Twice he pressed the trigger, but the pistol did not go off. At this point, another of the underwriters came in; Clive requested him to fire the pistol through the window. It worked perfectly. Puzzled, Clive once more decided that his life was needed for some great purpose. His attitude changed. He mixed with his fellow-workers, took more interest in his work and in his surroundings, and began to write detailed letters home about his activities.

In September, 1746, Madras was taken by a French force under Dupleix, who attacked from Pondicherry. The Governor and most of the English traders were taken prisoner, but Clive and his friend, Edmund Maskelyne, disguised themselves as natives and escaped to Fort St. David, an English Settlement further down the coast. Edmund Maskelyne was the brother of Clive's future wife.

At Fort St. David it was obvious that if the East India Company were to continue trading in the Madras area, it must have protection against the French, for Dupleix made it plain that he intended to drive them out. An experienced Army Officer named Stringer Lawrence was appointed as commander of Fort St. David, and Clive volunteered to serve under him. The misfit clerk had found his niche; Lawrence recognised him to be a born soldier and in 1748, as an Ensign, Clive took part in the siege of Pondicherry, a retaliatory measure led by Admiral Boscawen.

The complicated management of the English forces in India at that time seems incredible. The Company maintained its own army, consisting of native troops and white officers, most of whom, like Clive, were Company employees with no military training whatsoever. But, since this Anglo-French engagement was seen as a part of the War of the Austrian Succession, the Government was prepared to send out reinforcements. These, having been brought by the Navy, were commanded by Admiral Boscawen, who was relatively ignorant of land fighting. Further confusion arose because the local native rulers, seeking their own ends, frequently changed their allegiance. They also quarrelled among themselves and sought French or English help, whichever would bring them the greater advantage.

Under such conditions it is not surprising that the English did not succeed in taking Pondicherry. Major Lawrence was captured by the French but soon released when in 1748 the Treaty of Aix-la-Chapelle brought the war to an end. Clive returned to his desk, and for the next seven years the English and the French Companies in India observed one another uneasily, hoping to seize an opportunity to turn the local feuds to their own advantage.

During this break in hostilities Clive laid the foundation of his own private fortune. He went into partnership with Robert Orme, an English merchant; together they traded very profitably between Bengal and the Coromandel coast, and had it not been for Dupleix and the Indian princes, Clive would probably never again have seen military action. Dupleix, however, had set his heart on French domination of the European trade with India. To achieve this end, he had to get rid of the English trading stations, so he intervened in the Nawabs' disputes, siding with this one or that in the hope of alienating them from the English and so making as much difficulty as possible for the British East India Company. For the next fourteen years, the hostility between the English and the French in India was to be affected by involvement with the policies of various Indian rulers.

In 1750 two Princes, Chunda Sahib and Mohammed Ali, each claimed to be Nawab of the Carnatic. The French supported the former, the English the latter, who was immobilised in his fort at Trichinopoly by Chunda Sahib's forces. In the absence of Lawrence in England, an abortive attempt had been made by the English to capture Trichinopoly, and its failure had added greatly to the contempt in which they were already held by the Indians. Clive realised that, if the Company were to survive, Chunda Sahib must be replaced by Mohammed Ali. There was a great shortage of officers when Clive applied to rejoin the Company's Army, and he was given the rank of Captain. He suggested that, while Chunda Sahib was concentrating most of his troops on the siege of Trichinopoly, the English should act boldly and capture his capital, Arcot, which had been left virtually undefended.

The plan was agreed upon, and on 6th September, 1751, Clive set out for Arcot in command of a small force. Just after they had started, the monsoon broke and for sixty miles the march continued through a violent tropical storm. When Clive and his men reached Arcot, soaked but unharmed, the superstitious defenders surrendered the city without any attempt at resistance. Chunda Sahib, however, was less gullible. He promptly sent a relief army led by war-elephants and staffed by French officers. For two months Clive was besieged in the fort, but eventually he routed a full-scale attack, largely by his skilful deployment of field-cannon which sank a raft on which a large detachment of the assailants was attempting to cross the moat. The cannonade also caused

the elephants to stampede, injuring their own followers. The commander-in-chief, Chunda Sahib's son, fled, leaving Arcot in English hands. Clive, leaving a strong garrison behind him, returned to Madras, where he was allowed to make preparations for the relief of Mohammed Ali in Trichinopoly.

Early in 1752, as Clive's commander, Stringer Lawrence took charge of the attack on Trichinopoly. It is interesting that Clive, always so quick to resent any slight, never questioned the authority of Lawrence. The two men understood one another, and Lawrence, recognising Clive's military

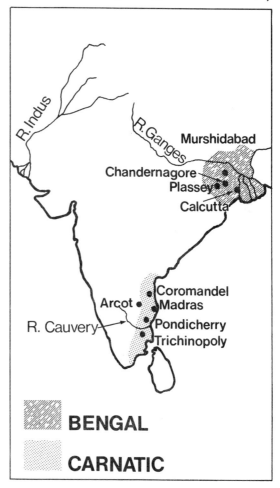

India at the time of Clive.

33

genius, gave him a free hand.

Trichinopoly was captured after a confused night of fighting on Seringham Island, in the Cauvery River. There were two temples on the island, which the English and the French, supported by Indian troops, used as hiding-places. At one point Clive dashed into a small pagoda filled with French troops. Although he was alone, he managed to convince them that they were surrounded by his army, so that they surrendered on the spot. Later in the night, he was slashed across the face by an Indian armed with a knife. Weak from loss of blood, he went over in the dawn light to the temple where the French were hiding, to offer them terms. A soldier fired at him twice, killing the two men who were supporting him as he walked, but Clive himself was uninjured. This third escape from death convinced him that he was invulnerable.

Mohammed Ali was freed and he and Chunda Sahib each ruled a portion of the Carnatic. Mohammed Ali gave Clive an Indian name, "Sabut Jung", meaning "The Valiant in War", and this became his title among the Indians. Although there was now an opportunity to break the French power in the Carnatic for good and all, Clive could not take it; the war between the princes was over, so he had no further excuse for attacking their French allies. Besides, he was ill: a form of blood-poisoning resulted from the wounds he had received at Seringham Island and he also contracted malaria. As soon as he became convalescent he was given home leave.

But before he sailed for England, Clive married, and the story of his marriage is as incredible as the plot of any sentimental romance. He, Sabut Jung, tough soldier and moody businessman, fell in love with a picture!

He had always maintained his friendship with Edmund Maskelyne, with whom he had escaped from Madras seven years before. One day, Maskelyne showed him a miniature of his younger sister, Margaret, a pretty, fragile-looking girl who, when the portrait was made, had been about fourteen years old. Clive thought about her constantly, and sent her messsages by her brother, eventually beginning to write to her himself. He told Edmund that there was no other woman whom he would wish to marry, and finally the two young men persuaded her parents to let her come out to India on a visit to her brother.

She arrived at Madras just after the capture of Trichinopoly, and when she first met Clive he was ill and bore on his face the unhealed scars of the knife-wounds received at the ambush on Seringham Island. Their four-month courtship reminds one irresistably of Othello and Desdemona:

> She loved me for the dangers I had passed,
> And I loved her that she did pity them.

But the marriage of Robert Clive and Margaret Maskelyne was destined for greater happiness than that of Othello and Desdemona. They never ceased to love one another; when they were apart, she was constantly in his mind; when he was rejected and took refuge in drugs, she remained steadfast. She did not re-marry after his death. During forty-two years of widowhood she never ceased to defend his name from slanderous attacks.

In 1754, however, this unhappy time was far away. She was seventeen, he twenty-nine, when they arrived in London. Clive was rich and bought a town house in Berkeley Square where he lived with considerable ostentation. The Directors of the East India Company presented him with a sword of honour, its hilt set with diamonds, in recognition of his services. It is in keeping with Clive's character that he refused to accept it unless a similar gift were made to Major Lawrence, his superior officer. Clive was loyal in his friendship as he was bitter in his hatreds. He always acknowledged his debt to Lawrence, and when the older man left the Company's service Clive augmented his pension by £500 a year.

The old quarrel with his father was made up. Clive paid off a heavy mortgage on the Styche, paid for the house to be rebuilt on a much grander scale, and provided handsome dowries for all his sisters.

He made enemies, however, both among military men and officials of the East India Company. There were many who laughed openly at his naive delight in spending his money. All in all, he was not sorry to return to Madras the following year, a Lieutenant-Colonel and Deputy Governor of Fort St. David, the Company's strongpoint for the defence of Madras.

He found Madras peaceful. Dupleix had been recalled to France, but the Indian Nawabs were still plotting against one another, and the French fomented the plots.

In 1746 the ruler of Bengal, Suraj-ud-Daula, decided to drive the English traders out of his dominions. Unlike the traders at Madras, those at Calcutta had never had occasion to defend themselves against either the French or the Indians. When they heard that the Nawab was advancing with a considerable army, the majority fled. Those remaining were captured and imprisoned in a cell in the garrison prison—for ever known as the Black Hole of Calcutta. Of 146 captives, only 23 survived and these were paraded in chains through the Indian city of Murshidabad, then set free to make their way to safety as best they could.

When this news reached Madras, the Company decided to send Clive with an army to re-capture Calcutta, and punish Suraj-ud-Daula. Calcutta was easily taken—the city was virtually deserted. But Suraj-ud-Daula went into hiding; he realised that he now had a powerful and furious enemy to deal with. It would be better to bide his time and try to make terms.

At this point, news came from Europe that France and England were again at war, and Clive knew that his army would be needed for the defence of Madras, but Calcutta was also vulnerable, not only to a French attack from their fort at Chandernagore but also to Suraj-ud-Daula, who would certainly return as soon as he was sure Clive was safely engaged elsewhere. Chandernagore was quickly taken, but it seemed impossible to pin down the Nawab and his vast army.

Clive decided to copy Dupleix's tactics and make use of Indian intrigue for his own ends. He knew that Suraj-ud-Daula had a rival, Mir Jafir, who had a considerable following in court circles. He offered to support Mir Jafir in a bid to overthrow Suraj-ud-Daula, in return for his promise to give the English East India Company a monopoly of trade in Bengal. Involved in the plot was an Indian merchant, Omichand, who threatened to inform Suraj-ud-Daula of this agreement unless his silence was bought at a price of about £300,000.

Calculating that it was reasonable to meet a blackmailer with blackmail, Clive had two copies of the agreement made. The copy shown to Omichand, incorporating his bribe, was afterwards destroyed; the real document sent to Mir Jafir made no mention of the merchant. One member of the Bengal Council refused to sign the false copy and Clive forged his signature. In later years his enemies made much of this equivocation.

On 23rd and 24th June, 1759, Clive defeated Suraj-ud-Daula and his French allies at the Battle of Plassey. Mir Jafir, now Nawab of Bengal, showed his gratitude and bestowed on Clive land and gifts worth £160,000; there was prize money to be shared out among the soldiers, and the East India Company's assets would be doubled by the increased revenue from Bengal.

The prize-money caused trouble, for the army officers refused to share it with the small number of naval officers who had fought beside them. Clive turned on them in fury. If they persisted in their refusal, he said, he would see that the prize-money was withdrawn; he had negotiated for it, he would withhold it. The army gave in meekly and the prize-money was shared, although some officers held it against him.

By 1760, the French threat to British trade in India was broken, and Clive returned to England. He was rich, he was famous, he expected further reward, either to be made a General or a Peer of the Realm. For Margaret he bought diamonds and rubies; he was received by the King, and in 1762 the Queen stood godmother to his baby daughter. He was elected Member of Parliament for Shrewsbury, and bought a town house there and also a country estate at Walcot, in the south of Shropshire. But he was disappointed to receive only an Irish peerage, the name of which he changed in order to style himself Baron of Plassey.

But the years in India had broken his health, and while he was ill—modern psychiatrists would agree that he had a mental breakdown—his enemies in the East India Company and the army acted against him. He was accused of obtaining money from Mir Jafir by unjust means. There were rumours of corrupt trading in Bengal, and for this, too, he was blamed. In 1765 he was ordered to return to Bengal and ensure just dealings there.

Ill and sullen, Clive went. He knew in his own mind that the province was too vast for the Company to administer; it should be ruled by the Government. But he dealt firmly with corrupt officials, both British and Indian, alienating many by his ruthlessness and impartiality. On his return to England in 1767, his enemies were ready for him.

The Chairman of the Directors of the East India Company, Laurence Sulivan, led a personal attack on him in Parliament and pressed it relentlessly for six years. Clive was again accused of dishonesty and treachery.

The Omichand treaty was brought up, and the forgery of a signature. It was stated that he had acquired his fortune by plunder and oppression, exploiting the Nawabs for his own ends. Eventually, after an open debate, a motion censuring him for fraud and embezzlement was narrowly defeated, and a resolution carried "That Lord Clive did at the same time render great and meritorious services to his country."

The campaign of vilification preyed on his already disturbed mind. He suffered physical pain, too, from a stone in the bladder, and to relieve this he took ever-increasing doses of opiates. He became melancholy, sitting alone in his rooms in Berkeley Square in a silence from which not even Margaret could arouse him.

In November, 1774, at three o'clock in the afternoon, his valet found him dead in his bedroom, whether from a stroke or an overdose of opium, taken deliberately or accidentally, is not certain to this day.

That night, his body was taken as quickly as possible to the Styche, where it was buried in the little Parish Church of Moreton Say. No stone marks the grave of the man who conquered India; his only memorial is a tablet set in the wall of the church, recording his name and dates of birth and death, and, by way of an epitaph, the Latin inscription, 'Primus In Indis'.

Richard Reynolds 1735–1816

Richard Reynolds.

Before the Industrial Revolution changed the face of the North of England and the Midlands, it made a quiet, almost unnoticed beginning in Shropshire, in a well-wooded valley between Shrewsbury and Bridgnorth, where the Severn flows swiftly through a gorge. Geographically, the area was favourably situated for the needs of small industry at a period before the advent of heavy mechanisation. The Severn provided a ready means of transport to and from the port of Bristol. There was abundant timber from which charcoal could be made for smelting; soon, small seams of coal and ironstone were found in the hillsides.

To this district (locally known as "the Dale" and later Coalbrookdale) came, in or about the year 1690, Abraham Darby, an ironfounder of Bristol. He made iron pots, and from this small beginning grew the Coalbrookdale Company, which remained in the hands of Abraham's descendants until 1922. The recent vogue for industrial archaeology had revived interest in the work of the first three Darbys—each of whom bore the family name of Abraham. Their furnaces at Blist Hill have been excavated; examples of their work in wrought and cast iron may be seen at the Industrial Museum at Coalbrookdale.

The second and third of the Darbys each died before his heir was old enough to assume control of the Works, so a manager had to be appointed. Each of these managers, Richard Ford and Richard Reynolds, married a Darby daughter, so the family relationships were close. The Darbys, the

Fords and the Reynolds were all members of the Society of Friends, or Quakers, and their religious beliefs had a considerable effect on their conduct of business affairs.

More is known about the personality of Richard Reynolds than of anyone else in the Coalbrookdale hierarchy. He and his family were given to letter-writing and keeping diaries, and because these papers have been preserved we have a very clear picture of Reynolds as a man, and of life in Coalbrookdale between 1756, when he first went there, and 1804, when he eventually retired and returned to his native Bristol, though he continued to make frequent visits to the Dale. He was a man whom everyone respected, who combined a shrewd business acumen with a sincere religious faith, a sense of humour and a deep love for all living things. Of himself he said, "My talent is the meanest of all talents, a little sordid dust. But as the man in the parable who had but one talent was accountable, I also am accountable for the talent I possess".

Richard was born in Bristol on 1st November, 1735, the only son of Richard and Jane Reynolds, both members of the Society of Friends. His father was an ironmerchant of considerable means, but he instilled into his children a belief in the virtues of economy. Young "Dicky"—this was always his family nickname—was sent away to a boarding-school at Pickwick, in Wiltshire, at the tender age of five-and-a-half, and was educated there for nine years. He records that he made the journey by carrier's cart, and one is inevitably reminded of the young David Copperfield. But Richard Reynold's schooldays were happy; his schoolmaster, Thomas Bennet, was his father's friend and aroused the boy's interest in Latin, Greek and History. Richard enjoyed his History lessons so much that he was for a time very eager to become a soldier, an ambition quickly discouraged by the Society of Friends.

Coalbrookdale.

38

Two events od his schooldays appear to have made a lasting impression on him. He was allowed as pocket money the sum of 2d. each week, but sometimes, like all schoolboys, he borrowed from his mates, but resolved soon afterwards never again to be in debt. He also told a lie at school—and this was a thing he always scorned. He was wrongly accused of some trivial misdemeanour and Mr Bennett threatened to whip him unless he admitted to it. So he confessed to something he had not done, in order to avoid punishment, and in after years related the story contemptuously to his children, for he despised cowardice.

By the end of his school career, Richard's interest in Classics was so developed that he would have liked to go to Oxford. But his father believed that every man should learn a trade, so in 1750 he apprenticed his son to a Bristol grocer, William Fry, also a Friend. From Fry he learned the economics of a business concern, details of imports and exports, management and accounting, which stood him in good stead later in his career. During this period of apprenticeship he also developed a love of outdoor life and nature which he never lost: indeed, he became a pioneer of conservation; no shooting or trapping was allowed on his land at Coalbrookdale, and this not to maintain a game preserve for the owner, but because he could not bear to destroy life.

Richard paid his first visit to Coalbrookdale in 1756, on business for his father, who was in the habit of buying pig-iron from Abraham Darby. Abraham Darby (the second) was a prosperous man; besides carrying on his father's trade in cast-iron household utensils, he had established a foundry at Ketley, where there was a coal-mine and another at Horsehay. He employed a large number of workmen, whom he treated with the fairness typical of the Quakers. The young Reynolds was impressed with what he saw, and developed a

great respect for Abrahm Darby. He paid several visits to Coalbrookdale, and in 1757 married his host's elder daughter, Hannah Darby. As a wedding present Abraham gave him a one-third share in the New Works at Ketley, which involved him in organising the colliery there, establishing steam engines at Horsehay and supervising the construction of wooden rails along which trucks of coal could be dragged to the blast furnaces.

The young couple settled in a substantially built brick house at Ketley, known as The Bank House, and their brief marriage was a very happy one. Hannah kept a diary of her domestic doings and she seems to have been fully occupied, as the following extracts show:

> *Tuesday (3rd. February, 1761) Kill'd a pig.*
> *W.—Kniting.*
> *Th.—Making Pork Pyes. Dickey at the Dale.*
> *Fr.—Cuting out shirts for Dickey. Will brewed the small bere.*
> *Sat.—Began to make Dickey's shirts. Tapt small bere.*

In March of the same year the house was decorated and whitewashed, and she was busy spring cleaning. They frequently visited her father at the Dale, and both her family and her husband's came to Ketley. But in 1762 Hannah caught measles from a friend whom she helped to nurse. She developed a chill, and on May 24th Richard's own diary laconically records "My Wife died of the Measles being but four days ill". At twenty-seven he was a widower with two children, a son aged four and a girl just one year old.

The following year, Abraham Darby died. His eldest son, another Abraham, was only thirteen and Richard Reynolds was asked by Mrs Darby and other shareholders to become manager of the Works during the term of her son's minority. This duty he carried out faithfully for the next five years, removing to Coalbrookdale in order to supervise the furnaces, deal with the accounts, and to see that young Abraham was fully conversant with every aspect of his inheritance.

It soon became obvious to Richard that his own children needed more attention than he was free to give them, and towards the end of 1768 he re-married. His second wife, Rebecca Gulson, was also a Friend. She became an affectionate mother to little William and Hannah, and later to her own three sons. But it was Hannah—nicknamed "Moley"—who was her father's favourite child.

Under Richard Reynolds' management the Works expanded and prospered, despite a period of economic depression which came at the end of the Seven Years' War. By 1766, the supply of timber from the woods surrounding Coalbrookdale had been almost exhausted, and this led to difficulties in making charcoal for smelting. Coal from the mines at Ketley and Dawley was used to heat the furnaces for pig-iron, but was not suitable when the more malleable wrought-iron was produced, as chemicals from the coal caused the metal to crack. At that time Reynolds had at Coalbrookdale a particularly skilful foreman named George Cranage, who, with his brother Thomas, experimented with a new furnace in which the iron did not come into contact with the coal, but only with the flames. The result was a new type of wrought-iron which retained its original strength. Characteristically, Reynolds insisted that the process be patented in the names of the Cranage brothers. Its direct result was to put the Coalbrookdale Works ahead of all others in the manufacture of wrought-iron articles.

In 1767 there was a considerable amount of iron in store at the Works, and it occurred to Reynolds that it could be utilised to make rails for the wagons which carried finished iron goods from the Works to the Severn. The wooden rails in use at the time wore out quickly and frequently cracked, so that a great deal of the workmen's time was taken up in repairing them. The iron rails proved so durable and successful that he had all the wooden ones replaced, and by the end of 1768, when Abraham Darby (the third) came of age, the Company possessed more than twenty miles of iron rails—the first in the country.

Once the young Abraham Darby was established, Richard Reynolds gradually withdrew from the management of the Works, although he remained for many years one of the principal shareholders and became the financier of the Company. In 1769 he instituted and supervised the construction of a towing path so that the barges could be moved more easily up and down the river. He had family connections with the tin-plate industry in South Wales, and in this way increased his personal wealth. He became a very rich man, but he was never ostentatious, preferring to use his money for the benefit of others.

In 1775, when the War of American Independence was at its worst, Abraham Darby refused to make any forms of armaments. Others were less scrupulous; the ironfounders of the Midlands were soon short of iron for weapons and it became known that the Coalbrookdale Works had iron to sell. Reynolds could have named almost any figure, but, true to his principles, he refused to profit by war, so he invariably asked his customers to suggest what seemed to them a fair price, and accepted it without any haggling.

Between 1777 and 1781, the Coalbrookdale Works became engaged upon its most famous project—the construction of a bridge over the Severn, made entirely of iron. The bridge was needed, for so much in the way of goods and raw materials had to be ferried to and fro across the river, with time-consuming loading and unloading, that a quicker route would save the Company thousands of pounds. The actual casting of the ribs of the bridge was done at Coalbrookdale. The construction of the stone abutments on which it was to stand proved difficult, for the Severn is very liable to flooding—engineers engaged upon the repair of the bridge two hundred years later encountered the same trouble. However, on January 20th, 1781, the *Shrewsbury Chronicle* reported:

The cast iron bridge over the River Severn between Madeley Wood (near Coalbrookdale) and Benthall was opened on New Year's Day last; since which time great numbers of carriages, horses and foot passengers have daily passed over the said bridge, the roads leading to and from it being nearly completed.

Ironbridge.

Though the Ironbridge—the first of its kind in the world—was built by Abraham Darby, there is no doubt that Richard Reynolds would be involved in its construction. One account of it, written in 1789, opens with the words "Coalbrookdale is one mile long, and the property of Mr. Reynolds and subscribers. Over the Severn in this Dale was laid in 1779 a bridge of cast-iron, the whole of which was cast in open sand . . ."

In 1784, Richard Reynolds was engaged in active and lively correspondence protesting at the proposal to levy a tax of 2/- on every ton of coal at the pit head. He pointed out to Earl Gower, President of the Council, that such a tax would result in a decrease in trade and consequently unemployment, not only in Coalbrookdale but everywhere in the kingdom where iron goods were manufactured. Four years later, he was trying to get through Parliament a Bill permitting the construction of a canal connecting the Works at Ketley with Shrewsbury. This project took some time to get underway but was eventually completed by Thomas Telford, then County Surveyor for Shropshire, in 1800. But after this his concern with the Works became less active. When Abraham Darby (the third) died in 1789, Richard Reynolds devoted more and more time to his private concerns.

The home life of the Reynolds family was always governed by the same principles of integrity and generosity which formed the basis of Richard's public activities. He insisted that all his children should be educated at home; perhaps memories of the little five-year-old boy who travelled to boarding school in the carrier's cart affected his decision. Their tutors, whom he interviewed personally, were scholarly and well-mannered. Once engaged, they were well-paid and treated as members of the family circle. He was interested, too, in the education of other children. During his period as manager he financed the building of a school at Ketley and, when he found that the parents of his workpeople withdrew their children as soon as they were old enough to make a contribution to the family income, he actually paid a bonus to any man who was prepared to allow his youngsters to attend school. At Madeley he handed over a substantial sum to John Fletcher, the Nonconformist preacher, to help him establish a similar school there.

He had a great affection for all children, and his gentle firmness quickly won their confidence. While he was living at Ketley he cultivated a large, walled garden. Every summer, at a time when the soft fruit was at its best, he would set aside one day when all the local children were allowed to wander in his garden freely, to pick whatever fruit they fancied. This, at a time when fruit was an almost unknown luxury to working-class children, was a rare privilege; the Ketley children always referred to the day on which they were licensed to pillage the Bank House garden as "Gooseberry Day".

Loving an open-air life himself, he was always eager for others to share this pleasure, and arranged an annual picnic on the Wrekin for his entire household, relatives, friends and servants. On Lincoln Hill, near Madeley, he had walks constructed so that his employees and their families could enjoy the woodlands and the views. Some of these "Workmen's Walks" as they were called, are in use to this day. He was a great believer in the axiom that people would work better if they were happy and comfortable. The Coalbrookdale employees were well housed at a nominal rent, and comfortable accommodation was provided for any of the Company's servants who became too old or ill to work. There were few accidents at Coalbrookdale, but if a man did have the misfortune to be injured Reynolds always undertook financial responsibility for the victim and his dependants.

Richard Reynolds also loved animals. As a young man he rode well, and always kept riding-horses for himself and his children. The Coalbrookdale area is hilly, and when he was driven to Shrewsbury in his chaise he always insisted that the horses should be led, slowly, up any steep incline.

He took great pleasure in Hannah's company, and after his withdrawal from active management, until her marriage, she was constantly with him. But he was too generous to monopolise his daughter. She loved housekeeping, so he had a little cottage built for her in the woods, where she was allowed to stay for several days at a time, with only her personal maid as companion, and organise her own house. This was a rare privilege at a period when an unmarried daughter was never allowed to go away from home unless under the constant supervision of an older relative.

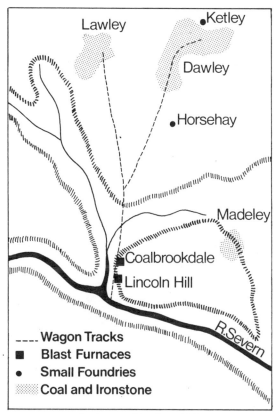

Sketch map of Coalbrookdale.

In 1786, Hannah married William Rathbone and went to live in Liverpool, and both her father and mother (she always thought of her step-mother as "Mother", for she was too young at the time of her real mother's death to have any memory of her) missed her. Visits were frequent. The entire Reynolds family travelled a great deal, usually on horseback. At one time, by way of entertaining a Quaker family from Pennsylvania, they took them on a tour of Wales which lasted a fortnight—a very strenuous undertaking at the end of the eighteenth century, when country roads were bad and accommodation worse.

When Hannah began to be occupied by the demands of her own children, the Reynolds adopted a young Quaker girl named Priscilla Gurney, a distant relative of Mrs. Reynolds, who assumed the duties of a daughter and showed great affection towards both Richard and Rebecca Reynolds. They on their part put no more restrictions upon her freedom than they had upon that of their daughter. Priscilla would occupy Hannah's cottage in the woods, and her adopted father bought for her a horse, which she named Serena.

Priscilla had a cousin named Elizabeth Gurney, one of seven sisters. This branch of the Gurney family were not Quakers, although Elizabeth was interested in the Faith. At Priscilla's earnest request, she was invited to visit her at Coalbrookdale, and years later recorded that it was while in the Reynolds home that she "first felt called to be a light to the blind, speech to the dumb, and feet to the lame". About a year after this visit she married a member of the Fry family at Bristol, and is known to History as Elizabeth Fry, the pioneer of prison reform.

His family were very anxious for him to have his portrait painted, but he always refused, for as a Quaker, he had a very literal belief in the sanctity of the Ten Commandments, and considered that the making of a portrait would break the prohibition put upon making a "likeness of anything in Heaven above; or in the earth beneath, or in the waters under the earth". But his sons invited a miniature-painter to come into the garden at night, and make a sketch of him while he was sitting in his study, reading by candlelight. Needless to say, a picture made in these conditions was not very successful, so Reynolds at last allowed himself to be persuaded to sit for a painter. He insisted that, in the portrait, he should be holding a Bible in his hand and that his favourite books should be shown in the background. His children were well-pleased with the portrait, especially Hannah, into whose possession the original eventually came, but he himself was always uneasy about it.

At the end of March, 1803, he became very ill; influenza was diagnosed and he was confined to bed. His wife caught the infection from him and died after a short illness, though Reynolds himself recovered. They had been married for forty years.

The year 1803 was a sad one for him, for in the summer William, his son by his first marriage, also died. Richard Reynolds decided that he would leave Coalbrookdale and return to his native Bristol, and this he did in the Spring of 1804. Here he took a small house in James' Square, and Priscilla Gurney and his cousin, Sarah Allen, looked after him. He busied himself with Quaker affairs and, like Elizabeth Fry, took an interest in prison reform. A rich man with simple tastes, he spent large amounts of money in helping prisoners to make a fresh start, often paying for a man's passage to America, where other Friends would employ him, or releasing debtors, for whom he felt great pity, by paying their creditors and giving them sufficient money to maintain their families until they were once again in a position to support them.

In 1816 he was ill again, and when he recovered insisted on visiting Ketley, where his son Joseph now occupied the Bank House. Hannah and her children joined the family party, and although the old man was in good spirits he confided to Joseph that he felt certain that this was the last occasion on which the family would all be together. His premonition was true; later in the same year Joseph received a message from Priscilla to tell him that his father had died on September 9th, in his eighty-second year.

Richard Reynolds served three generations of the Darby family as friend and partner, and lived to see the birth of a fourth Abraham Darby. During his lifetime the Coalbrookdale Works grew from a forge at Coalbrookdale, partially supplied with fuel from a colliery at Ketley, to a very large concern, connected by canal to Shrewsbury and with its own private sources of iron ore at Lawley and Dawley in addition to that conveyed by barges up the Severn. He carried out faithfully his obligation as trustee and manager for young Abraham Darby, and by applying the principles of the Society of Friends to his relationships with his workers he made the Coalbrookdale foundry a concern on which many modern industries, both publicly and privately owned, could profitably be modelled.

Henry Hill Hickman 1800–1830

Henry Hill Hickman. Oil on canvas, copied by Herman Solomon from the original.

At the beginning of the nineteenth century surgery was still a rough-and-ready business, and the surgeon's place the lowest in the medical hierarchy, coming after the physician and the apothecary. In London, the work of John Hunter and the founding of the Royal College of Surgeons in 1800 had done something to elevate surgery in public esteem, but in the country, a surgeon who visited a great house was entertained in the housekeeper's room, whereas the physician was the friend of the family. Training in surgery was rudimentary; the usual practice was to apprentice a boy to a surgeon. There was no systematic teaching of anatomy—officially, the London hospitals were given the bodies of four condemned criminals a year for public dissection. Anaesthesia and asepsis were undreamed of, so in the majority of cases the unfortunate victim of the operator died, either from shock or from gangrene. Small wonder that the surgeon was regarded with horror.

By the year of Waterloo, however, things were changing—at least, in London. Men like Sir Charles Bell and Sir Astley Paston Cooper, by their skill and brilliance as teachers and practitioners, brought about a reversal of public opinion. In defiance of the law, they taught anatomy and dissection privately, obtaining their subjects from local graveyards, as did Dr Knox in Edinburgh. The secrets of the human body were known to them; they understood that many internal ailments could be cured by surgery. But such operations were impossible to perform, for no-one could survive the pain and shock involved.

We do not know why Henry Hill Hickman, a farmer's son from Lady Halton, Bromfield, near Ludlow, decided to become a surgeon. His father was a tenant farmer on the Earl of Plymouth's estate, his mother a farmer's daughter. He was the seventh child of a family of thirteen, born on 27th January, 1800. We have no details of his education, although there is a strong local tradition that he was a pupil at Ludlow Grammar School. Neither is it known how he obtained his basic training. Probably he was apprenticed to some local surgeon, accompanying him on his rounds, watching him at work and sometimes being allowed to perform such simple operations as blood-letting, the removal of warts or lancing boils. A promising pupil would be sent to a medical school to complete his studies, and Henry Hickman was a medical student at Edinburgh from 1819 to 1820. He matriculated in November, 1819, but left Edinburgh without obtaining his degree. He must also have

spent some time in London, for he was admitted as a Member of the Royal College of Surgeons in May, 1820. In the Autumn of that year he started to practise medicine and surgery in Ludlow, having a house in Corve Street. It is interesting to note that, almost two hundred years before the Welfare State was envisaged, he hung in his window a printed card stating that he was "At Home, every Tuesday, 10 o'clock to 4, for the purpose of giving Advice Gratis to the Poor and Labouring classes".

Many of the leading surgeons in London treated the poor for nothing, or permitted their students to do so, but it was by no means a common practice in country districts.

At this time, Henry was engaged to be married. His fiancee, Eliza Hannah Gardner, was the only daughter of Benjamin and Catherine Gardner, of Leigh Court, near Worcester. Benjamin Gardner was a substantial farmer, and Leigh Court is an historic

Corve Street, Ludlow.

46

house, once the property of Elizabeth I's favourite, the Earl of Essex. The Gardners were a local family, and in all probability they, like the Hickmans, were tenant farmers. How and when Henry and his wife met is not known, but they corresponded while he was a student at Edinburgh, and were married at Leigh on 21st June, 1821, "with consent of parents", for the bride was only seventeen years of age. Their marriage was duly entered in Leigh Parish Register, which can be seen at Worcester Record Office. Five people signed as witnesses—though no Hickman name is there; the bride's signature is adorned with a large blot, although her handwriting is clear and firm.

Between 1820 and 1824, while he was in practice at Ludlow, Henry Hickman carried out a series of experiments on anaesthesia. There are several reasons why he could have become interested in the subject, for it was a possibility which currently engaged considerable speculation in medical circles. But it is strange that an obscure country practitioner, who had never, so far as is known, been connected with any of the few teaching hospitals, should have performed and recorded these experiments. One wonders what aroused his curiosity and led him to follow up his idea with such painstaking tenacity. His hypothesis was wrong, yet he came so close to the correct solution of the problem of pain and its inhibiting effect upon major surgery.

At this time Sir Humphry Davy, Britain's leading scientist, was President of the Royal Society. This brilliant man studied many branches of science, among them the effects produced by the inhalation of various gases. This was never one of his serious interests, but he is recorded as observing, in 1800, that headaches and toothache could be relieved by inhaling nitrous oxide, and that in the future this gas might be used to lessen pain during surgery. Neither he nor anyone else appears to have attached any importance to the remark at the time, but it is quite possible that Hickman knew of it. Davy was a frequent visitor to the Ludlow area; he was a close friend of Thomas Andrew Knight, the owner of Downton Castle, which stands on the banks of the Teme, between Bromfield and Ludlow. Knight, a horticulturalist, was also a member of the Royal Society. A wealthy man, able to indulge his hobby, he imported various sub-tropical shrubs which he cultivated in his gardens. He and Davy shared an interest in fishing, and Davy visited Downton every year, to fish in the Teme. Hickman certainly knew Knight, though probably not as a personal friend—the social distinction between the landowner and the surgeon would have precluded this. But Knight was the man to whom he looked for help when he was ready to publish the results of his experiments.

Another local man, Thomas Beddoes, had advocated the inhalation of gases to relieve certain lung complaints. Beddoes, a contemporary of Hickman's father, was born at Cheney Longville, a village in the Ludlow area. He became a medical practitioner at Shifnal, then moved to Bristol, where he founded his Institute of Pneumatic Medicine. Henry Hickman lived in Shifnal from 1824 to 1827, but by that time Beddoes was dead, though Hickman must have known something of his work.

Probably he first began to consider the idea of anaesthesia while he was at Edinburgh for he appears to have been a sensitive man, stating that he "often longed for some means whereby the fears of patients could be tranquillised and their suffering relieved". The operations which he would perform would be simple by present-day standards—amputations, lancing of abscesses and tumours, and "cutting for the stone", dreaded since the days of Pepys. For any of these a short period of unconsciousness, not more than a few minutes, would have been sufficient.

Hickman tried Carbon Dioxide—he called it "Carbonic Acid Gas". His method was to cause some small animal, usually a puppy or a kitten, to inhale the gas. Then, while the creature was unconscious, he would amputate an ear or a tail. In each case the animal suffered no pain, there was very little bleeding, it regained consciousness when taken out into the air and soon recovered completely. It is an interesting sidelight on Hickman's character that he states in his records that every one of his animal "patients" was, for some reason or other, condemned to be destroyed; having risked their lives for his own purposes he refused to put them in danger of death again, but allowed them to live out their normal span.

These experiments occupied him during 1821, 1822 and 1823. He recorded every one accurately and methodically—it is obvious that he had a scientific mind—and their success led him to the conclusion that "Carbonic Acid Gas" could be used to render a human patient unconscious for a short period, sufficient for a minor amputation or incision, but here he came to a stop. He was a young, unknown doctor, bound by the nascent ethics of his profession. He could not set a human life at risk, not even his own. What he needed was the backing of authority, for leading surgeons or scientists to develop his experiments. For himself he asked nothing; he sought only the further exploration of his thesis for the ultimate benefit of human sufferers. The man whom he felt would be able to help him in this project was Knight of Downton, the local squire. To him Hickman sent a detailed account of his experiments, together with an explanatory letter, in February, 1824.

Exactly what followed is not clear, but Hickman seems to have expected Knight to pass on his work to Humphry Davy, who would put it before the Royal Society for consideration. Knight appears to have done no such thing, and his treatment of the young doctor gives an impression of carelessness surprising in a man interested in scientific research. But it must be remembered that from 1823 onwards Davy was far from well. His mental powers were failing; in 1824 he was sent on a voyage, ostensibly with some scientific purpose but in reality to remove him from England for a time. Shortly after his return he died. It is likely that Knight, believing Hickman's work to be of an ephemeral nature, decided not to bring it to the attention of Davy while the latter's health was so uncertain.

Hickman, however, expected support for his theory and to have it considered by a scientific body. By 1824 he was living, with his wife and two children, at Shifnal. Here, he had his work privately printed in pamphlet form, under the title "A Letter on Suspended Animation". On the title page he stated that the letter was originally addressed to T. A. Knight, Esq., of Downton Castle, "one of the presidents of the Royal Society", and that it was "read before them by Sir H. Davy".

Only one of these pamphlets is still in existence. It is at the Wellcome Museum of Medical History, in London; the words "read before them by Sir H. Davy" have been heavily deleted by a series of ink strokes. Moreover, the paper was never read: the records of the Royal Society contain no reference to it.

Did Henry Hickman himself deface the phrase which would have meant so much to him—the official recognition by a leading scientist of the value of his research? His disappointment must have been bitter, but he still did not abandon his ideal. On June 3rd, 1825, he sent a copy of his letter to the *Shrewsbury Chronicle*, a local newspaper. The title page was omitted, but the Editor published an account of the experiments, prefacing it by stating that:

Doctor Hickman, of Shifnal, has published a letter shewing that Suspended Animation may be

Henry Hill Hickman, experimenting on suspended animation. From a water colour by Richard Cooper.

safely employed during Operations on Animals with a view of ascertaining its probable utility in Surgical Operations on the Human Subject.

He added that he was publishing details of Hickman's work "In the hope of furthering the writer's desire for liberal experimental enquiry".

The unlucky Hickman gained nothing from his communication to the *Shrewsbury Chronicle*. Subsequent editions carry no mention of it, although in 1826 a writer using the pseudonym 'Antiquack' ridiculed its content in an acrimonious letter published in the *Lancet*.

Henry Hickman's tenacity was remarkable. To us, it is obvious that he was on the wrong track; his "Carbonic Acid Gas" would have caused the death of any patient to whom it was administered over a prolonged period. But to him, and to his contemporaries, anaesthesia was a dream which seemed beyond fulfilment. Not only the patient, but the surgeon also, dreaded any operation; many of the greatest surgeons in

London prayed with their patients before the ordeal. Sir Charles Bell has recorded that he could neither eat nor sleep when he knew that he was to operate the following day. Here was an unimportant country practitioner who believed that he had discovered a means to end this terror, and no recognised authority was prepared even to give him a hearing. At this point, most men would have given up; Hickman went on.

As London would hear nothing of his theory, he decided to seek support in Paris, where the Académie Royale de Médecine was internationally famous for its progressive attitude towards medical research. How he found the means to take this step is not known. It is a reasonable supposition that he raised the money by selling his practice at Shifnal, for his wife and family went to her relatives at Bromyard, near Worcester, at this time. On 21st April, 1828, he wrote her a lively and enthusiastic description of his journey to France, during which all the passengers except himself were very seasick. His success in making himself understood in a foreign language gave him a naive delight; he was full of the magnificence of the French capital, where he hoped that, if all went well, she might soon join him.

At this period France was permeated by a strange atmosphere, both in politics and in culture. After the traumatic experiences of the Revolution and the Napoleonic Empire, the populace had been returned to the Bourbon regime. Of Louis XVIII, brother of Louis XVI, it was truly said that he had "learned nothing, forgotten nothing" during his years of exile. He was succeeded by his younger brother, Charles X, in many ways so reactionary that his supporters were known as the "Ultras"—even more retrograde than the pre-revolutionary monarchists. Yet, in some respects, Charles was remarkably liberal in his outlook. He was a notable patron of the Arts and took a great interest in Science. Though uninformed himself, he was prepared to encourage scientific developments, and to him Henry Hickman wrote for support.

What can have given him the idea of writing a personal letter to "His Most Christian Majesty, Charles X, King of France"? And how did he know how to phrase such a letter? For it is presented neither in the language of a scientist nor of a country doctor, but that of a courtier. He briefly states his position and outlines his thesis, seeks the King's permission to demonstrate his idea before the French medical and surgical schools in order to secure their co-operation, and begs to present his "Book" (presumably a full account of his experiments) to the King.

There are two possible links between Henry Hickman, of Shropshire and Charles X, King of France; both are tenuous.

In 1828, some English artists were among those employed on the restoration of the Royal residences in Paris. Two of them, the Glover brothers, had relations living in the same part of Worcestershire as Hickman's wife's parents, so he could well have obtained an introduction to them. Also he might, when a boy in Ludlow, have come into contact with Napoleon's brother, Lucien, who lived in England from 1810 to 1814.

Lucien was something of a black sheep in the Bonaparte family. Genuinely inspired by the ideals of the French Revolution, he objected strongly to his brother's Imperial designs, while Napoleon in his turn objected strongly to Lucien's wife. So Lucien took refuge in England, where he rented a country house in Ludlow. It is not very likely that he and Henry Hickman ever met, but it is perfectly feasible that friendships were formed between Ludlow people and Lucien's French servants, and out of such a contact could have come Hickman's idea of going to Paris. This, however, is merely speculative.

Hickman remained in Paris for at least two months, staying at a small hotel in the

Rue des Férmes des Mathurins, not far from La Madeleine, which was then unfinished. From here he wrote his letter to the King; here he waited for the Committee of the Académie Royale to invite him to speak before them; here, his hopes must have eventually faded.

The French medical authorities appear to have treated him with as much indifference as their English counterparts. His account of his work was duly passed to a M. Géradin, who referred it to a sub-committee. The only supporter of the theory was Baron Larrey, ex-Surgeon General of Napoleon, who believed in the possibility of painless amputation because he had himself, during the Retreat from Moscow, amputated the limbs of men who were so numbed by the cold that they were not sensible of what he was doing.

Larrey was, in his day, the greatest surgeon in France, and the fact that he remained a member of the committee of the Académie Royale de Medecine during the reign of Charles X proves that the medical world still held him in high esteem. But politically he was certainly not in accord with the tide of opinion in Court Circles. Possibly his support did Hickman more harm than good, for there is no record of any further communication between the Académie Royale and the British doctor.

Hickman returned to England and resumed practice, taking a house at Tenbury Wells. In 1830 he died, only thirty years of age. He was taken for burial to his birthplace, Bromfield, where his grave may still be seen in the village churchyard.

The cause of his death is unknown, and the local paper carried only a simple announcement of it. His young widow appears to have been left very little, for she opened a girls' school in her house at Tenbury, where she remained with her young family. The eldest child would have been barely nine years old at the time of the father's death.

By 1847 the use of nitrous oxide as a means of anaesthesia in dentistry had been discovered, and the Americans, Morton, Wells and Jackson, were all claiming the distinction of being first in the field of painless surgery. While their work was being discussed by various European medical bodies, M. Géradin of the Académie Royale de Medecine recalled a letter which he had received some fifteen years previously, in which an English physician had put forward a similar claim. At the same time, in England, a Dr. Dudley wrote to the Editor of the *Lancet*, strongly urging that Hickman was the true pioneer. This Dr. Dudley had already been in touch with Hickman's widow, asking her to send him any of her late husband's papers still in her possession, so that he could ensure that credit be given where it was due. She seems to have lost or destroyed them, for he wrote more than once, begging her to search. But there the matter ended, and to this day, outside the world of medical science, Hickman's name remains unknown.

A century after his death, however, the medical fraternity paid him belated tribute. After a memorial service at Bromfield church, attended by many members of the Royal College of Surgeons, a stone plaque was unveiled. It is set in the wall inside the church and carries the following inscription:

A.M.D.G.
Henry Hill Hickman, Member of the Royal College of Surgeons.
Born at Lady Halton, in this parish, January 27th., baptised in this church, January 30th., 1800.
Died at Tenbury, April 2nd., buried in this churchyard April 5th., 1830.

This tablet is placed here at the initiative of the Royal Society of Medicine, as a Centenary Tribute to the earliest known pioneer of anaesthesia by inhalation.

Honour a physician with the honour due to him.

Thomas Telford 1757–1834

Thomas Telford as a young man; before him is the design for the front elevation of Bridgnorth Church. Artist unknown.

The purist may contend that Thomas Telford has no legitimate claim to a place in a book concerned with Shropshire personalities, and the contention is, up to a point, valid. Telford was neither a Salopian by birth, nor by education; he spent only about five years as a resident of the County town. His varied career involved him in projects in England, Scotland, and Ireland as well as in Sweden. His place of retirement—if the word retirement can be applied to him—was London and he was buried in Westminster Abbey. Why, then, do Salopians regard him with a proprietary air, even to the extent of giving his name to the new town now being built in the eastern part of the county? The answer lies in the fact that it was in Shrewsbury that Telford first had the opportunity to prove himself as an engineer, that two of his greatest projects, the Ellesmere Canal and the Holyhead Road, were centred on Shropshire and its borders, and that he maintained a close connection with the County until his death. It is not possible, in a short biographical sketch, to describe in detail all Telford's major undertakings; this account will be confined to his work as it affected Shropshire, which was the first county to recognise his greatness as an engineer, and to acknowledge him after his work had been in eclipse for more than a century. For Telford was pre-eminently a builder of roads, bridges and canals; during the railway era his work was of little value, but since the decline of the railways he has come into his own once more. Modern motor traffic speeds over roads which are still virtually Telford's roads; his basic technique of road-making remains that of the modern engineer.

It was in August, 1757, that Janet Telford, wife of an Eskdale shepherd, gave birth to her only child, a son, who was christened Thomas. The Telfords were a border clan—"Jaimie Telfer of the fair Dodhead", hero of the ballad of the harried man, was a direct ancestor of Thomas. The roots of the family were set in rolling, upland country, and it was in similar mountain landscapes that this child's destiny lay. His father, however, did not live to celebrate his son's first birthday. He died when the baby was only four months old, and Mistress Telford and her son left their cottage and went to live with relatives at Westerkirk, the nearby village. Here, thanks to the generosity of his uncle, young Thomas was educated at the parish school. The boy was industrious and had little time for play, for his mother was poor and during the holidays and out of school hours he earned what he could to augment her income by helping out neighbouring crofters and shepherds, sometimes, during the lambing season, spending nights alone on the hillside, with only the ewes for company.

His childhood made him self-reliant and reserved, for he had little time to indulge in casual friendships. He was proud too, and conscious of his dependence upon his uncle, although the latter seems to have been a kindly man with a strong sense of family duty. He made only one close friend at school, Andrew Little, with whom he maintained a correspondence which was kept up until Andrew's death in 1805. Little became a surgeon, but was obliged to abandon his profession because he became partially blind while still a young man. So he returned to the Border country and became master of the village school at Langholm. When Telford became rich and successful he did not forget his old friend. He once wrote to Little that, now he had money, it had become his chief care to ensure that his mother and his friend should never be in want.

After leaving school Thomas Telford was apprenticed to a stonemason, but his master ill-treated him, so he ran away. Once more his uncle came to his rescue. He realised that the boy, though headstrong, was intelligent and deserved a proper training. He apprenticed him again, this time to a skilled craftsman, Andrew Thompson, a master mason at Langholm. Thompson taught him well, and through him Telford obtained work on the estate of the young Duke of Buccleuch, who had in hand a project for building new roads and farmhouses on his estate. Through Thompson, too, he met Miss Pasley of Langholm, who, impressed by the knowledgeable young journeyman sent to carry out some repairs to her house, gave him the freedom of her bookshelves and introduced him to major works of literature. As a result of this contact he acquired a love of poetry which he never lost.

One of Telford's 'prentice pieces was a tombstone for his father, which still stands in the graveyard of Westerkirk. It bears the inscription:

IN MEMORY OF JOHN TELFORD WHO, AFTER LIVING 33 YEARS AN UNBLAMEABLE SHEPHERD, DIED AT GLENDINNING, NOVEMBER, 1757.

He must have accomplished this piece of work in order to please his mother, of whom he was very fond.

In 1780, Thomas Telford left Langholm for Edinburgh, where the building of Princes Street and the New Town offered good prospects for a stonemason. But in 1782 he had an opportunity to go to London. Sir James Johnstone of Westerhall, the employer of Telford's uncle, wanted a reliable man to take a horse to his brother in London. The uncle suggested that Thomas should go, and so, at twenty-four, the ambitious young man set off for the South, riding another man's horse and with his own few possessions packed into a saddlebag. He also carried a letter of introduction from his old friend Miss Pasley to her brother, a London merchant.

In London, Miss Pasley's letter brought valuable contacts. Her brother introduced him to Robert Adam and Sir William Chambers, two of the city's leading architects, and Chambers immediately offered him employment as a master-mason at Somerset House, which was then in course of construction. Telford was proud of his work on Somerset House, but his self-confidence was such that, as he wrote to his friend Andrew Little, he felt "born to command" and was convinced that all the London workmen were ignorant. He himself spent all his spare time in study—Literature, Mathematics, Draughtsmanship—anything which came his way, he was prepared to master. When Somerset House was finished, he and some of his fellow-masons were sent to Portsmouth, to build a commissioner's house, a new chapel, and some offices on the dockyard. This was a very important opportunity for him, for he was instructed to superintend the work—probably Sir William Chambers recommended him. He remained at Portsmouth for eighteen months, during which time Sir William Pulteney once more came into his life.

Sir William, James Johnstone's brother was one of the wealthiest men in England. He was M.P. for Shrewsbury and, needing a residence in the town, had bought the old Castle. Shrewsbury Castle, however, was not habitable; Sir William had purchased a derelict ruin. He remembered the young architect from his own native Eskdale and offered him a free hand to convert it into a suitable dwelling-house.

Telford arrived in Shrewsbury at the end of 1786, and January 1787 found him hard at work. Something more than their Borderland heritage must have drawn the

Sir William Pulteney, M.P.

two men together, for Pulteney's was not an attractive personality, but Telford held him in high regard, and Pulteney in his turn seems to have respected the integrity of his young protegé, showing him so much favour that the townspeople mockingly referred to him as "young Pulteney". Probably the trait which linked them was a common ruthlessness of purpose, so that, once set upon a project, neither man was prepared to give it up and any obstacles in his path were removed.

Pulteney persuaded the Shropshire County Council to create a new post and offer it to Telford—Surveyor of Public Works for the County of Salop. So he was the first County Surveyor, and a very thorough one. In Shrewsbury he had to superintend the building of a new Gaol and a new Infirmary. Parts of his buildings are still in use, which says much for Telford but little for our Penal System or our National Health Service.

In 1788, he carried out the first excavations on the Roman site of Uriconium. His methods would horrify a modern archaeologist, but thanks to his sense of reverence for the past, local farmers were no longer allowed to use the ancient city as a stone-quarry. Telford brought to light "a set of Roman Baths and a tesselated pavement". Of these he made careful plans, having first found out all he could about Roman methods of building. What he had actually discovered, although neither he nor the local antiquarians realised it for some years, were the hypercausts, or heating chambers, under the floors of a series of buildings. From then on Uriconium was recognised as a valuable historical site; although, owing to lack of money and a natural reluctance to disturb valuable agricultural land, the city has still not yet been fully excavated, at least it lies there, undisturbed, for archaeologists of the future.

Telford drew up plans for the reconstruction of Shrewsbury High Street, and in 1792 and 1793 built new churches at Bridgnorth and at Madeley. In 1788 the Churchwardens of St. Chad's Church, Shrewsbury, consulted him about repairs to the church roof, which was leaking. An extensive examination of the fabric revealed the need for very extensive repair work, which the Churchwardens refused to undertake, accusing Telford of creating work for himself. Three days later the church tower collapsed, destroying almost the entire building and leaving what Telford himself described as "a very remarkable, magnificent ruin".

It was as County Surveyor to Shropshire that Telford built his first bridge—Montford Bridge, a few miles North-West of Shrewsbury, on the Holyhead Road. This was completed in 1792, and in the following year he built the Tern Bridge at Cound. In all, Telford was responsible for the construction of more than forty bridges in Shropshire, and

some of these are still in use.

But in 1793, although he remained county Surveyor, his attention was turned towards a new project, the construction of the Ellesmere Canal. This developed into a major engineering feat, involving complicated planning and the erection of two enormous aqueducts. The year 1793 was an important turning-point in Telford's career. Before he began work on the canal he was merely a stonemason turned architect; after its completion he may correctly be described as the first modern civil engineer.

At that period, canals were seen as a cheap and direct means of industrial transport. River transport was used, but the Severn was notorious for flooding and, therefore, unreliable. A plan was formed, backed by the Darbys of Coalbrookdale and John Wilkinson of Willey, together with the Wedgewoods, to cut a series of canals linking the Mersey, the Dee and the Severn, and so providing an easier outlet to the sea for Midland industrial products than the treacherous voyage to Bristol via the Severn.

The official promoters of the plan were the Members of Parliament for Shropshire and Montgomeryshire, and because their first public meeting was held at Ellesmere, the canal was given the name of the Ellesmere Canal. Telford, apparently at the suggestion of Abraham Darby and William Reynolds, was appointed as "General Overlooker"—which meant that he was responsible for the construction work. His appointment was opposed by a number of the shareholders, who had their own candidate, William Turner, in mind, but the wealthy ironmaster John Wilkinson backed Telford, so Turner's claims were overruled.

The canal took twelve years to complete and eventually Telford's original plan was modified, as while England was involved in the Napoleonic War it was decided that it was too costly to take the canal across the Ruabon Mountain. The section between Chester and

Ellesmere Port was soon completed, as was the section from Ellesmere to the Severn. Telford then began work on the next stage, which involved carrying the canal, by means of two great aqueducts, over the Vale of Llangollen and the Ceiriog Valley at Chirk.

Telford had already constructed a small aqueduct. In 1795 he was asked to complete the Shrewsbury Canal, which linked the town to the coalmines at Ketley. At one point the Canal had to cross the River Tern and this Telford accomplished by the use of an iron trough cemented into a low stone bridge. He applied this principle to the construction of his aqueducts at Chirk and at Llangollen, but in order to maintain his water-level above these deep valleys, the trough had to be carried on stone piers at least 100 ft high. Chirk aqueduct was completed in 1801 and the tremendous Pont Cysyllte at Llangollen, in appearance not unlike the Pont du Gard at Nimes, in 1805. Pont Cysyllte was officially opened by a procession of barges which passed across it on 26th November, 1805. Telford himself always referred to this section of the Canal as his "stream in the sky".

As a result of his work on the Ellesmere Canal, Thomas Telford became world-famous as a canal engineer. At the invitation of Count Von Platen he went to Sweden, where he drew up plans for the Gotha Canal. Between 1803 and 1822 he was responsible for the construction of the Caledonian Canal, and he advised or planned many other inland waterways in England.

At the beginning of the 19th Century, Irish Members of Parliament were experiencing difficulty in attending sittings of the House. First came the crossing to Holyhead, then, after a bumpy ride across the Island of Anglesey, they had to traverse the dangerous Menai Strait by ferry. They then made their way, along roads virtually unchanged since the Romans first laid them down, to Chester or Shrewsbury, and on to London by routes little better. They complained bitterly about the arduous journey and in 1815, at the instigation of Sir Henry Parnell, the Member for Queens County, Telford was instructed to make a survey of the entire length of what is now known as the Holyhead Road.

He had already made a similar survey of

Section of the Shrewsbury Canal, showing Telford's embankment and bridge.

some roads in the Highlands of Scotland but this task occupied him and his two assistants for two years. His report, put before a Parliamentary Commission in 1817, showed that between London and Wellington the road could be made serviceable by a series of minor alterations—cutting corners, easing gradients and re-surfacing. But between Shrewsbury and Holyhead the road needed re-laying, as did the North Wales Coast route from Bangor to Chester. In his opinion, the Shrewsbury to Holyhead route was worth the expenditure involved, and he advised the Commission to buy out the seven Turnpike Trusts which controlled it and to deal with the complete stretch as one unit. Because of his successes with difficult roads in the Highlands they took his advice, although he warned them that it would be a long and difficult task—his estimate of the cost of making the section from Chirk to Holyhead was £53,000 per annum for five years.

The Holyhead road took fifteen years to make, although fast coaches were able to use it before it was completed. Telford began on the most difficult section, west of Llangollen, and his friend, the poet Robert Southey, gave an exact description of laying a road. He worked as the Romans had worked, and one is led to speculate on how far he was inspired by memories of his early excavations at Uriconium.

His method, according to Southey, was "first to level and drain; then, like the Romans, to lay a solid pavement of large stones, the round or broad end downwards, as close as they can be set; the points are then broken off and a layer of stones, broken to about the size of Walnuts, laid over them, so that the whole are bound together; over all a little gravel".

The iron felloes of the era, exerting pressure on such a surface, rapidly packed down the gravel so that it became perfectly

Toll House on the Holyhead Road at Montford Bridge.

smooth, and the good drainage, combined with a generous camber, prevented any accumulation of rainwater or mud. A century later, however, it quickly became obvious that pneumatic tyres did not have the same effect, and resurfacing was a constant necessity.

One of the major undertakings of the project was the bridging of the Menai Strait, which Telford did by means of a suspension bridge. Massive towers were erected at either side of the Strait, to which the suspension chains were to be attached. The links for these chains, each nine feet in length, were made at Upton Magna by the Shrewsbury ironmaster, William Hazeldine, and their tensile strength tested by a machine specially installed for the purpose at his Coleham Works in Shrewsbury. These huge links were taken to the Ellesmere Canal Wharf at Weston Lullingfields, ferried along the canal to Chester and thence by boat to the Strait. On 26th April, 1825, all shipping was stopped in the Menai Channel while they were hoisted into position by block and pulley. Telford himself was at the top of one of the towers to supervise the operation, and crowds gathered on the Anglesey and Caernarvon shores to watch. When the last of the vital link pins had been driven into place, a great cheer went up, and three of the workmen actually crossed the Strait by walking along one of the chains—a highly dangerous exploit as the iron links were only nine inches wide!

The Holyhead road became one of the most famous coaching roads in England, but with the advent of railways the stage-coach gradually disappeared and long-distance travel by road declined. Now, in the age of motor transport, it carries more vehicles than ever before, and apart from its surface and minor alterations it is still fundamentally Telford's road. He remained its official surveyor for the rest of his life, and inspected it personally every other year.

Thomas Telford's life as a civil engineer involved him in constant travelling, and it was not until he was sixty-four years old that he bought a permanent home. In 1821 he purchased No. 24, Abingdon Street, opposite to the Houses of Parliament. Here he enjoyed entertaining his friends, among whom were not only engineers but the poet, Thomas Campbell and the nephew of his old friend Andrew Little. Telford himself never married—he appears to have been too much involved in his work. Southey had nicknamed him "The Colossus of Roads"; by virtue of his majestic size a Colossus has to stand alone.

During Telford's lifetime engineering had become a recognised profession, and some of the younger engineers in London formed themselves into a society at first devoted to purely social purposes. But in 1820, the members decided to make their Society more formal. Official rules of membership were drawn up, permanent premises acquired, and in 1820 the Institution of Civil Engineers invited Telford to become its first president. To this he consented, and by his active membership and international reputation he added considerably to the status of civil engineering as a profession.

In 1825, Telford began work on his last canal, the Birmingham and Liverpool Junction. This, cut between Wolverhampton and Nantwich, brought him once more into Shropshire. It promised to be an easy task, for the flat country of North Shropshire, Staffordshire and Cheshire presented no problems in the way of levels that could not be solved by locks. However, one obstacle presented itself, which almost broke Telford's spirit and left the canal uncompleted at the time of his death. This was the construction of Shelmore Great Bank.

The new canal met with opposition from the landowners through whose property it was to be cut, and its bitterest opponent was Lord Anson of Norbury Park, who flatly refused to sell to the Company any part of his game reserves in Shelmore Wood, which occupied a small triangle of land between Newport, in Shropshire, and Gronsall, in Staffordshire. Because of Lord Anson's attitude, Telford was forced to modify his plan and make a great embankment to carry the canal beside Shelmore Wood. The basic soil was a sticky clay and every spell of wet weather softened and loosened the bank, so that tons of it slipped away. For four years Telford and his assistants worked on Shelmore Great Bank, and four winters' rains undid the work completed every summer. The rest of the canal was ready for use, but its two halves could not be united because of the morass at Shelmore. The Birmingham and Liverpool Junction became the most costly canal ever cut in England.

In 1830 Telford, who was then 73 years of age, fell ill. He recovered, but it was obvious that his vigour was gone. Moreover, he became deaf, and to one of his quick intellect this was an unbearable affliction. When he came for the last time to Shrewsbury he was a frail old man, his disability making it difficult for him to communicate or to take part in conversation. Nevertheless, at the request of the Borough Council he gave advice on the preservation of the Welsh Bridge, which had been damaged by floods, went on to take a last, bitter look at Shelmore Great Bank, and agreed that, in view of his own ill-health, a young man named William Cubitt should deputise for him as the Company's engineer and try to complete the canal. But Shelmore Great Bank defied Cubitt also, and it was not until six months after Telford's death that the canal was navigable.

Telford returned to Abingdon Street, deaf, frail and lonely. He had no close friends left for he had outlived them all. His will, drawn up a few months before his death in 1834, shows how he remembered those earlier friendships by bequests to sons and widows of former companions and, most

Thomas Telford as an old man.

touching of all, £1000 to the Minister of the parish of Westerkirk and £1000 to the Minister of the parish of Langholm, in trust, for the purchase of books for a library. Miss Pasley had long been dead, but her influence had lasted all his life, and he was determined that other ambitious lads in his birthplace should have ready access to books.

His death, at the beginning of the steam age, caused his fame to be rapidly eclipsed, and many who passed his monument in Westminster Abbey had no idea why he should be buried there. It is only now, when railways in their turn have had their day and once again roads carry the bulk of transport, that his greatness as an engineer is fully realised.

Shropshire, now very sensible of the the beneficial results of his work on the commerce of the county, has given his name to a new "overspill" town, at present being constructed to accommodate industries and workers from Birmingham and Wolverhampton. It is certainly fitting that Telford New Town is sited between his first canal, made to connect Shrewsbury with Ketley, and the scene of his one spectacular failure, Shelmore Great Bank.

John Mytton 1796–1834

John Mytton at Halston, painted by an unknown artist.

The genius of Telford, the philanthropy of the Darbys and the dedication of Agnes Hunt are known to few outside their own county, but the crazy exploits of the worthless John Mytton are almost as celebrated as the brilliance of Charles Darwin. The man was a wastrel and a fool, who during his lifetime dissipated a great fortune and brought his estate to ruin, yet despite his faults his friends spoke well of him, his tenants, servants and electors grieved at his death. He typified the era of license and scandal into which he was born—a period during which the excesses of the sons of George III had brought the Monarchy into such disrepute that, at the accession of Victoria in 1837, England was on the verge of becoming a republic. "Mad Jack" Mytton was as wild as any of the wild young aristocrats who were his contemporaries, yet he was generous to a fault and was his own worst enemy. His biographer and friend, C. J. Apperley, "Nimrod", was certain that, towards the end of his life, Mytton was insane, and he was probably correct in this assumption. But it seems ironic that, more than a century after his death, Mytton, who did nothing of value, should remain one of the best-known Shropshire characters.

He was the descendant of a very old Shrewsbury family, whose name had appeared on the burgess rolls of the town, generation after generation, since 1373. Myttons had also represented the town in Parliament. In the time of Elizabeth I Edward Mytton acquired the manor of Halston, between Ellesmere and Oswestry. Halston—the name is a corruption of "Holy Stone"—was originally the property of the Knights of St. John, who were dispossessed by Henry VIII. The land was fertile and well-wooded, and its new owners amassed a considerable fortune. In 1690 John Mytton's ancestor built for himself a very elegant country house, and between 1766 and 1768 its interior was re-designed in the fashionable Adam style. John Mytton's grandfather led the life of a typical eighteenth century gentleman, on land which had been in the possession of his family since Tudor times, and in due course the estate passed intact to John Mytton's father, who, unfortunately died before his heir was two years of age.

"Mad" Mytton was born on 30th September, 1796, and was brought up by a mother who spoiled him and by guardians who had no control over him whatsoever. His mother gave him his own way in everything, and by the time he was six years of age, he had got himself into so many scrapes that his uncle nicknamed him "Mango—King of the Pickles". His waywardness amused his mother at the time; years later, she saw the result of her over-indulgence.

When he was old enough, he was entered first at Westminster, then at Harrow, and was expelled from both schools for dis-obedience. As the heir to a considerable es-tate who was also a minor, he had become a ward of Chancery, and while he was at West-minster he had an allowance of £400 a year. Young John's expenses, however, amounted to double this sum. He was fourteen years old, but, hoping that the Lord Chancellor would forget his age, wrote to him asking for an increased allowance on the grounds that he intended to get married in the near future. The Lord Chancellor was less gullible than Mrs. Mytton, and his reply was brief and to the point.

"Sir", he wrote, "if you cannot live on your allowance, you may starve; and if you marry, I will commit you to prison".

John Mytton finished his education un-der a private tutor. He did not lack in-telligence, and had a natural aptitude for Greek, developing a real love and understan-ding of the work of Classical authors which he never forgot—at the end of his life, bankrupt and half-mad, he would still quote Homer and Sophocles. He could have become a scholar, but he also loved riding, hunting and shooting, and did not lack the means to enjoy these pursuits. His mother and his guardians wanted him to go to Oxford, but he refused point-blank, so the family Chaplain was asked to impress upon the young man the necessity of completing his education. He agreed to enter Christ Church on condition that he should read only the Racing Calendar and the Stud book, and ordered three pipes of wine to be sent to him there, but he never went into residence. When he was eighteen he was sent on the usual Grand Tour—cut short, in his case, by the escape of Napoleon from Elba and the battle of Waterloo—and then returned to Halston to take up the management of his estate.

It is interesting to consider John Mytton as typical of a post-war period. After the Napoleonic Wars life in Europe went through a phase of unrest very similar to those which immediately followed the Wars of 1914–1918 and 1939–1945. The young "Bloods" who were Mytton's contem-poraries had much in common with the "Bright Young Things" of the 1920's and the "Teddy Boys" of the 1950's. They felt that they had been cheated out of the excitements of war-time and rebelled against society as they found it. They were determined to shock, and to shock others was John Mytton's ambition. He had to be the centre of attrac-tion. His tragedy was that, unlike the majori-ty of adolescents, he never outgrew this stage of development.

When he came of age he was a tall, stur-dy young man, with a pleasant face and, despite his boorish manners, an indefinable air of breeding. He was proud of his own strength and went out of his way to show contempt for physical comfort. Winter and Summer saw him out in all weathers, wearing thin shoes, unlined trousers of white linen and a light jacket. He would often ride more than fifty miles in a day, or would walk all day, bareheaded, in the hottest summer weather. One winter night, in order to demonstrate his hardiness, he stripped naked before crawling over a frozen pond, and lying for some hours in the snow, in wait for wild duck. He never needed to use a handkerchief, and he never wore gloves, for his hands did not get cold. In an age when tremendous meals were eaten as a matter of course, he was no gourmand, though he had a great weakness for nuts and once devoured eight pounds of filberts at a sitting. But he did become a heavy drinker, and by the time he came of age he was already consuming seven bottles of port a day without any apparent ill-effect, though several of his friends warned him that, if he persisted, the ultimate effect upon even his physique would be disastrous.

John Mytton very quickly gained a reputation for hare-brained tricks. Mytton could do anything with horses, whether riding or driving. He trained one of his carriage horses to rear up on its hind legs at his command, then sink slowly to the ground, without damaging the carriage. On one occasion he was buying a horse from a dealer at Meole, near Shrewsbury, and in order to try the animal's paces harnessed it with another to a light gig and drove both tandem. When they came to the turnpike gates at Hanwood, Mytton said to the dealer, "Is he a good timber-jumper?" The dealer expressed his doubts.

"We'll try him," said Mytton and giving the horse his head, struck him on the flank with his whip and set him at the turnpike gate. The horse cleared it in great style, but the other horse, Mytton and the dealer, were piled against the gate. The gig was badly damaged, but both men and the horses escaped unhurt.

Sometimes Mytton prevailed upon the driver of the stage-coach to allow him to drive from Shrewsbury to Whittington. On these occasions he invariably handled the team perfectly and never did anything which could cause risk to the safety of the passengers.

There were large stables at Halston, and Mytton kept about twenty hunters and race-horses, as well as his carriage horses. He also owned a pack of fox-hounds. One of his favourite hunters was named Baronet, and with this animal Mytton could do anything. He is said to have ridden him into Halston Hall, and up and down the great staircase. On one occasion, returning home after a day's hunting, night fell while he was still some distance from home. Both he and Baronet were cold and wet. He knocked up a local innkeeper and demanded a fire and refreshment for himself and his horse. Man and beast spent the night before the fire in the inn parlour, and next morning went on to Halston.

Mytton also had at this time a more unusual pet, a bear named Nell, which he had bought at Ellesmere from a travelling showman. Sometimes he would terrify his guests by bringing Nell into his dining room and riding her round the table.

He was given to practical jokes, which, though they amused him, caused considerable discomfort to his victims. On one occasion, having dined and wined well, he went for a stroll in his grounds. He encountered a beggar going up to the Hall. Instead of driving the man off his propery, Mytton tipped him handsomely and borrowed some of his clothes. Dressed in this tattered costume, he went to the back of Halston Hall and tried to beg from his own servants, who refused to give him anything more than the dregs of a barrel of beer.

"You fare too well", Mytton told them, "and get saucy in your places, or you would never offer a fellow creature such stuff as this".

The butler, hearing the uproar, came out and ordered the beggar off, but Mytton promptly knocked him down. The other servants then set the dogs on him, but the animals recognised their master and Mytton revealed his identity, compensating the butler with a guinea. (Surely he must have taken this idea from a tale of Robin Hood?)

He was fond of disguises and always ready for a fight. Once, after interviewing a man who had applied for a post as keeper, Mytton told him that he would give him the job if he could drive off a certain chimney-sweep who regularly came poaching on the Halston coverts. The keeper agreed to keep watch that night as a trial. The poacher eventually appeared and the man set about him. They fought for the best part of an hour, and the keeper was getting the worst of it when the 'sweep' pushed him off and revealed himself as Mytton, his face blacked and with shabby clothes. The man had done very well, he said, and gave him the job.

Tricks of this kind endeared him to his servants, but were frowned upon by the county gentry. It was time, he was told, to marry, to settle down, and to give Halston an heir. Mytton married twice. His first wife, Miss Emma Jones, was the younger sister of Sir Tyrwhitt Jones, of Stanley Hall. She was not strong, and died soon after the birth of her only child, a daughter. Mytton seems to

Halston Hall.

have grieved at her death, although he was bitterly disappointed at the sex of the child. After his wife's death he refused to have the little girl at Halston and until her father remarried she was brought up by Mrs. Corbett, of Sundorne Castle, near Shrewsbury.

His second wife, Miss Caroline Giffard, was related to the family of the Duke of Devonshire. She insisted on marrying Mytton, in spite of her mother's doubts that he would keep his promises to mend his ways and make her a good husband, and seemed willing to put up with his unstable behaviour. "I cannot help loving him", she confessed to a friend, "whatever he does". But Mytton became more wild as the years passed, and by the time he was thirty-five he was drunk more often than he was sober, and beginning to show signs of mental instability. He was insanely jealous of his wife, eventually confining her to one wing of Halston and refusing to let her speak to anyone but a servant of his own choosing. For a time, Mrs. Mytton seemed prepared to endure this, but at last his prolonged drinking bouts, coupled with the fact that he introduced into the Hall guests of an extremely dubious reputation, became more than she could bear. She managed to get in touch with her family, and with their help escaped from Halston while her husband was away from home. Her brother started proceedings for an annulment of the marriage, on the grounds that Mytton had been insane at the time of the wedding. The suit dragged on, and before it reached a conclusion, Mytton died. His heir, one of the children of this marriage, was brought up by his mother's family.

John Mytton became a Member of Parliament for Shrewsbury in 1819, though he never took his seat at Westminster. These were the days when votes could be bought, and the Mytton fortune allowed him plenty of scope. He made the Lion Hotel his headquarters, and, on being elected, was carried there shoulder-high by his supporters. However, when they reached the Hotel, Mytton, flown with success and very drunk, leaped from their backs and entered the Lion through a window. He was in the habit of staying at the Lion when in Shrewsbury, and proved a very tiresome guest; on one occasion, he terrified the staff by loosing two foxes in the dining room. However, as he invariably paid in full for any damage he caused, he was always welcome as a customer. Whatever his faults, no-one could accuse him of meanness.

His genius with horses led him to take an interest in racing, and sometimes he himself rode as a gentleman jockey. He began betting heavily, and losing heavily also. But, although his friends and his lawyer advised him that the Halston Estate could not stand losses on this scale, he refused to be warned. After his second wife left him, his wildness increased, and it was obvious that there was more than a touch of insanity in his behaviour. He took to drinking not port, but brandy; he gave money away lavishly, he gambled, he got into debt. Eventually, he became a bankrupt. The entire contents of Halston were sold to pay his creditors, but there was still not enough money and, rather than be put into a debtor's prison, he crossed the Channel and lodged at the Crown Hotel in Calais.

Here, Mytton once again met his old friend "Nimrod", who was staying in France at the time. "Nimrod" was horrified at the change in him. Although only in his middle thirties, he was tottering, round-shouldered and bloated. He seemed quite indifferent to the disastrous change in his fortunes, remarking carelessly that he would soon recoup his losses.

One morning "Nimrod" was roused by Mytton's servant, who begged him to come quickly, as his master was very ill. On reaching the Crown Hotel, he found Mytton in his bed, the skin of his breast, back and shoulders so badly burned that he could not bear the sheets to touch his flesh. He seemed to be quite delirious, for he explained to "Nimrod" that, the previous night, he had been kept awake by an attack of hiccoughing; in order to stop it he had set fire to his nightshirt, so that he would "give himself a fright".

The servant confirmed the story. He had saved his master's life by rolling him on the floor and then tearing the smouldering garment off him. When "Nimrod" asked whatever made him do such a silly thing, Mytton replied that he wanted to prove that he could bear the pain.

"Nimrod" sent for a doctor and the burns were dressed. He also sent for Mytton's mother, as his friend seemed to be very ill indeed. Sometimes he talked incoherently, constantly he drank, although the doctor had warned him that his constitution was so badly undermined that, unless he stopped drinking, he would be dead in a few days.

"I want to die", he replied.

However, when his mother arrived she managed to persuade him to relinquish the brandy bottle, and very soon, though obviously weak, he was on his feet again. At this point, an emissary from his lawyer appeared in Calais, bearing a somewhat garbled message, the gist of which was that if Mr Mytton would return to England and sign certain documents concerning the sale of his remaining un-entailed property, there would in all probability be sufficient money to settle his outstanding debts.

Back to England he went, drunk during the entire journey. He signed the documents, but there was not enough money to pay all he owed. So, in order to escape his creditors, Mytton went back to Halston, the one place where he was certain to be recognised.

Recognised he was, and arrested for debt. The ex-Member for Shrewsbury was taken to the county town and lodged in the town gaol. The gaoler, a man named Griffiths, owed his post to Mytton, who had recommended him in his more prosperous days. Griffiths treated him with great kindness, and Mytton told him on leaving that he had been very comfortable in Shrewsbury gaol. Before long, however, another writ was issued against him and he was transferred to the Kings Bench Prison in London. Here he died, from the combined effects of paralysis and gaol fever, on 29th March, 1834.

His mother had his body taken to Halston for burial, and all the gentry of North Shropshire attended the funeral, for Mytton's family name was still respected, though he himself was not. The ordinary people, however, remembered "Mad Jack's" exploits with admiration and many had reason to be grateful for his generosity. In Shrewsbury and in Oswestry, the shopkeepers closed their shutters as a sign of mourning. In Ellesmere, Whittington and Halston, the bells tolled all day. All along the road between Shrewsbury and Halston, men stood bareheaded to watch Squire Mytton pass for the last time. He was a fool and a lout, but his personality certainly left an impression which has survived the eroding years. To this day, among Salopians, the name of "Mad Mytton" evokes laughter which is half pitying, half admiring. Although he wasted a huge fortune and disgraced the name of his family, his faults are forgiven because he rode around his dining-room on the back of a bear, and set fire to his nightshirt in order to cure an attack of the hiccoughs.

Charles Darwin 1809–1882

Charles Darwin.

Charles Robert Darwin, the fifth child of Dr. Robert Darwin and his wife, Susannah, was born at The Mount House, Shrewsbury, on February 12th, 1809. Dr. Darwin was a wealthy physician, his wife a daughter of Josiah Wedgwood, the potter. They already had three daughters and one son, Erasmus; another daughter was born in 1811.

Charles was baptised at St. Chad's Church, and his early childhood appears to have been a happy one. He had the large garden of The Mount House to play in, and as both his parents loved flowers and shrubs he regarded an interest in botany as a normal part of life. His elder sisters kept pet animals and birds, and his father bred pigeons as a hobby. The beautiful Mount House pigeons were well-known in the town. Every summer the family went to North Wales for a seaside holiday, and the children became familiar with the environment of the shore. It was a perfect background for a naturalist.

Mrs. Darwin died when Charles was eight, and the eldest daughter, Caroline, took charge of the family. Amongst other duties, she taught the two youngest, Charles and Catherine, to read, but her brother's progress disappointed her. She found him obstinate and unwilling to learn. Dr. Darwin, aware of a slight family tension, sent him to a small day-school kept by Dr. Case, the minister of the Unitarian Chapel in High Street, who was a family friend, for Mrs. Darwin had been a Unitarian.

Like most boys of his age, Charles had at this time a passion for collecting things—shells, seals, coins and minerals were among his enthusiasms. He also went through a phase of collecting birds' eggs, though he was careful to take only one from any nest. He enjoyed fishing, but would not use live worms as bait, and when he began to collect insects he never killed any, but hunted carefully for dead specimens. This humane attitude was instilled into him by Caroline.

In 1818 Charles joined his elder brother, Erasmus, as a boarder at Shrewsbury School. Dr. Butler, then headmaster, was a leading Classical scholar, so the curriculum was devoted to the study of Latin and Greek; Mathematics was frowned upon, Science not taught at all. Neither of the Darwin boys found much of interest in this time-table, and Charles, more vocal than his brother, was openly bored by it. Dr. Butler disliked him, and when the fact leaked out that he and Erasmus were conducting experiments in chemistry in a converted garden-shed, the headmaster administered a sharp reproof. Charles considered this an injustice; when he became a public figure, he observed that his school had done nothing for his education.

Dr. Darwin had some sympathy with his sons. He arranged for Charles to have private tuition in Euclid, which he loved, revelling in its logic. He was anxious for one of the boys to join him in his practice. Erasmus had no inclination towards medicine, but Charles, with his qualities of observation and compassion already defined, seemed to have the makings of a good physician. So in 1825 he entered Edinburgh University Medical School. He was a reluctant student; the career did not attract him, but he was too kindhearted to disappoint his father. Besides, there was nothing he particularly wanted to do instead.

It was not long before his instinctive

Upper Form Room, Old School, Shrewsbury.

feeling that he would never make a doctor was confirmed. The anatomical lectures bored him and he was unable to overcome a revulsion for dissection. He attended only two operations, and these filled him with such horror that in neither case was he able to remain in the theatre until the surgeon had finished his task. Anaesthesia had not yet been discovered, and the agony of the patients remained in his memory for the rest of his life. When he was old he became a champion of the anti-vivisectionist movement; his reverence for all forms of life was such that he felt man had no right to inflict suffering on any living creature.

Other facets of his life at Edinburgh were more enjoyable. He made friends with Dr. Grant, a young demonstrator who introduced him to the theories of the Frenchman, Lamarck, on the beginnings of life. Speculation about the creation of life fascinated the intelligentsia of the time. Mary Wollstonecraft Shelley's novel "Frankenstein", dealing with the dreadful consequences of the creation by a scientist of a living man, had been published seven years earlier. Charles's own grandfather, Erasmus Darwin, had written two scientific poems about creation in which he, like Lamarck, dismissed the Bible story as it stood, feeling that the world could not possibly have been made in seven days, by a series of several acts. It was more likely, they thought, that the creator would have taken years to reach the height of perfection—Man—and that the intermediate stages of creation would have been connected. Charles was of course familiar with his grandfather's book, *Zoonomia*, and he and Grant gave careful consideration to this and to Lamarck, but dismissed both because neither could support his theory with facts.

Another of Dr. Grant's hobbies was Geology, then a very new science indeed. At that time, no-one realised how very old the Earth was. Geologists held two views about

rocks, fossils and stratification. Some said that all rocks were formed from sediment left by Noah's flood: the water receded slowly, and the various strata were nothing more than a series of tide-marks. Others insisted that the Flood was only one in a series of "catastrophes" which occurred while the Earth was in process of formation, and that after each catastrophe life became extinct, so new forms were created to replace the old. Fossils were obviously the remains of life-forms which had been destroyed by the catastrophes.

Darwin found both these ideas unconvincing. He remembered a Shrewsbury antiquarian showing him a curious stone, the "Bell Stone" (still to be seen in Shrewsbury), and telling him that there was no other rock of the same type in the area. Moreover, nobody could explain how the stone came there, nor ever would be able to find out. The incident impressed Darwin, who recorded later how he "meditated over this wonderful stone". He and Grant both felt that there must be some key to the mysteries of the rocks.

A humbler Edinburgh acquaintance was a negro taxidermist, whom Darwin found both pleasant and obliging. He taught him how to stuff animals and birds, an accomplishment which proved useful later, when he had to preserve his own specimens.

By 1828 it was abundantly clear to Darwin that he was quite unsuited to the profession of medicine. His father had to be told, and this presented difficulties. The relationship between father and son was a complex one. Dr. Darwin was a kindly man, but overwhelming in both his physical presence and his character. He was tall and broad, with a deep, reverberating voice. Charles loved him deeply, but at the same time feared him—apparently without real cause. The most probable explanation is that the son felt himself to be a disappointment to the father, and this feeling increased as he

H.M.S. *BEAGLE* IN THE STRAITS OF MAGELLAN
It was Darwin's experiences as naturalist on the voyage of the *Beagle*, a five-year surveying expedition round the world—and particularly the South-American fossils and birds—that led up to his life-work on evolution.

The 'Beagle'

grew older. It is typical of the situation that Charles persuaded Caroline to tell Dr. Darwin of his decision. It was not the first time she had acted as his emissary; whenever he needed money he would never ask for it directly, although he knew his father would not grudge it. Always he wrote to Caroline, who approached their father on his behalf.

Dr. Darwin was sufficiently generous to understand Charles's objections. He decided that his son should become a clergyman, so Charles entered Christs College, Cambridge, in the Autumn of 1828. The docility with which the young man agreed seems remarkable: probably he was ready to drift from one academic discipline to another because there was no form of training for the career to which his peculiar talents were suited. He spent three years at Cambridge, leaving with a B.A. in Theology, Euclid and Classics, but was not considered in any way outstanding. The person who influenced him most was quite unconnected with his own course of study. He was the Professor of Botany, John S. Henslow.

Darwin attended Henslow's open lectures, and joined his excursions in search of rare plants and insects. Henslow introduced him to Adam Sedgwick, the young Professor of Geology, although the latter's work did not seem of much importance to Darwin until his student days were over. But Darwin spent more time upon subjects which were not included in his course than he did upon theology.

Soon, he was again preoccupied with feelings of guilt, for he realised that the Church held no more attraction for him than medicine had done. Even Caroline would jib at breaking this piece of news. Characteristically, Charles put off the evil day and went on with his studies, but he tended to avoid his father at this time, spending most of his vacations at the home of his mother's brother, a second Josiah Wedgwood, known affectionately as "Uncle Jos". Uncle Jos had a country house at Maer, in Staffordshire. Here Charles found the atmosphere much freer than at The Mount House—Uncle Jos had not the dominant personality of Dr. Darwin—and he and his Wedgwood cousins went shooting, or for long country rambles.

It was Dr. Henslow, himself a clergyman, who made Charles face reality, persuading him when he left Cambridge to tell his father that he had no vocation for the Church. Dr. Darwin seems to have taken the news very calmly, for he raised no objection when his son left almost immediately with Adam Sedgwick, to study Geology in the Llangollen area. This tolerant attitude is more readily understood if one realises that no economic factors were involved. Charles had no need to earn a living; his father was well able to provide for him.

When he returned from Llangollen, Charles found a letter awaiting him—a letter, as he said later, which was to change the course of his life. It was from Henslow, and enclosed another from Robert Fitzroy, Captain of H.M.S. *Beagle*. The Admiralty was sending the *Beagle* on a surveying expedition to chart the coasts of South America and the Pacific Islands. Fitzroy, who was interested in natural history, had persuaded their Lordships that a naturalist should be included in the company, and the post had been offered to Henslow. He, feeling that it was work for a younger man, had recommended Darwin. At first, Dr. Darwin refused to allow Charles to go, but Henslow and Sedgwick persuaded him to change his mind, and in 1831 Charles joined the *Beagle*, for a voyage which was to last five years.

The voyage of the *Beagle* gave Charles Darwin a purpose in life, though his first experience of life on board proved a bitter disappointment. He was dreadfully seasick throughout the voyage; conditions on the ship were cramped, even though he was sharing the captain's cabin, and there were many points on which he and Fitzroy did not see eye-to-eye. One early bone of contention was the vexed question of slavery. Fitzroy upheld it; Darwin, conditioned by the Wedgwoods as well as by his own natural instincts, abominated it. After a shore excursion in Brazil he vowed that never again would he visit a slave-owning country. Years afterwards, the sound of a distant scream recalled to him the memory of a sordid little shack in Pernambuco, from which he heard the demented screaming of a beaten slave.

But Darwin enjoyed the voyage, for all that. He noted the geology of the Cape Verde Islands and South America, collected plants, animals and insects in the tropical forests of Brazil, observed the natives of Tierra del Fuego and survived an earthquake in Chile. Before leaving South America he packed up several crates of geological specimens which he sent to Cambridge, where his friend Henslow received them.

Next, the *Beagle* visited the Galapagos Islands, which are still a naturalist's paradise.

Here Charles was able to observe forms of life previously unknown to him. He timed the speed of the giant tortoises, which took ten minutes to walk sixty yards. He performed a post mortem on one of the giant lizards, proving that the creatures fed upon seaweeds. He took an especial interest in the finches of the archipelago, noting the varied shapes of their beaks—large and powerful on an island where seeds and small nuts grew plentifully, small and sharp where insects abounded. He puzzled over the fact that, in one small group of islands, the appearance of one species of bird varied in a manner best suited to deal with the food supply on the island where the individual lived.

Tahiti, New Zealand and Australia were also visited, and in the Autumn of 1836 the *Beagle* returned to Falmouth. Two days later, Charles was back in Shrewsbury, where he arrived late at night and slept at an inn rather than disturb his family.

There was no further doubt in his mind as to his future career, and he was elated to learn that both Adam Sedgwick and Captain Fitzroy had written to his father, praising his talent as a naturalist. Dr. Darwin no longer urged him to become a clergyman; the unsatisfactory son had found his metier at last. After a short visit to Uncle Jos at Maer, Charles took rooms at Cambridge, where he proceeded to write up his notes of the voyage and classify his specimens. He wrote other notes, too—not for publication. New ideas were simmering in his brain, but they must not be presented to the public until he had given them logical consideration and was certain he could support them with proof.

Charles Darwin, at twenty-nine, seems to have been at the peak of his physical powers. Tall and active, bronzed from the Australian sun, he was tireless. He wrote, lectured, divided his time between Shrewsbury, Cambridge and London. But, quite suddenly and unaccountably, this abundant vitality began to decline; he became a prey to migraine and bouts of sickness, to which he was subject for the rest of his life. No explanation has been discovered for his subsequent relapse into semi-invalidism. It has been suggested that the violent and continuous seasickness from which he suffered throughout the voyage of the *Beagle* permanently affected his mechanism of balance. Another possibility is that, while in South America, he contracted Chagal's disease; again, it is conceivable that his illness was neurotic in origin. (This last explanation is a very probable one, tying up with the inconsistencies of his character and the fact that, when fully absorbed in writing or experimenting, he was always well, although a crisis, like the death of his father or the storm following the publication of *The Descent of Man*, laid him low). But it is certain that, after 1838, he was never again a completely fit man.

In 1839 he married his cousin, Emma Wedgwood, Uncle Jos's daughter. The marriage, which delighted both families, was a very happy one. The young couple settled in London, and Charles devoted himself to writing and lecturing on Geology and Natural History, Emma to protecting and cosseting him. By 1842 his journal of the voyage of the *Beagle* and his account of the formation of coral islands had assured his place in the scientific world. That year he bought Down House, in Kent, which was to become his family home. He also began a draft for his *Origin of Species*, but put it away. It was not published until 1859.

For seventeen years Charles Darwin withheld his theory of evolution, although his facts were assembled and his book planned. Moreover, he was sufficiently certain of its importance to impress upon Emma that, should he die before it was written in full, she was to make sure that the draft was not destroyed. It is difficult for the modern reader to understand his hesitation; in actual fact, he must have fully realised what the book's impact would be. It would strike a major blow at contemporary religious belief, and Darwin, surrounded by such conventionalists as the Wedgwoods, his father and Henslow, shrank from the consequences.

We are so far from the circumscribed religion of the Victorians that many of their tenets now appear ridiculous. True, a few advanced thinkers discussed "catastrophes" and "connected" creations, but the majority of people firmly believed in the creation of the world as recorded in the Old Testament, with mankind as its culminating point, separate from the animal kingdom, "in the likeness of God". There were many who had even a date assigned to the event—4004 BC Darwin knew that his evolution theory would upset all this and, if carried to a logical conclusion, would destroy the concept of a personal Deity. He himself, he said later, abandoned that idea so gradually that he suffered no shock in so doing. But he knew that others would suffer, and his gentle nature recoiled at the prospect of becoming a storm-centre. He could write on other subjects; let evolution rest.

But he could not let it rest for ever. In 1858 he received a letter from a fellow-naturalist, Alfred Russel Wallace, outlining a similar theory. The issue could no longer be evaded. Darwin and Wallace produced a joint paper on evolution for the Linnaean Society. Wallace acknowledged that Darwin had explored the subject more deeply than himself, and had a prior interest. Darwin worked upon the notes he had kept secret for so many years, and in 1859 published *The Origin of Species by means of Natural Selection*.

His thesis was that there was no sudden creation, no separate creation of each species. All living things show a tremendous variety, even within the same species where variety is necessary for adaptation to a different environment. (The Galapagos finches were an example of this.) It was impossible for all these variants to be the result of innumerable separate acts of creation; they must have come about by means of gradual change or *evolution*. And this evolution was the direct result of the struggle for existence. Since all species produce far too many offspring, only those best suited for life in their environment would survive. Over a long period of time this natural selection would result in the appearance of new species, all descended from the same common ancestral type.

The storm which Darwin had foreseen broke with a vengeance. He had pushed home his argument with examples which any educated man could understand, and the Church, led by Samuel Wilberforce, Bishop of Oxford, denounced him as an atheist and a blasphemer. Darwin withdrew from the conflict. He had made his statement, let others wrangle. Gradually, the scientists triumphed, the Church retracted; the thinker of Down was acclaimed as a genius. But in 1871, the appearance of *The Descent of Man* opened the controversy again, for in this work Darwin definitely included Man as a product of the evolutionary process. Not only did he point out that, structurally, man and the anthrapoid apes bore a similarity too obvious to be ignored; he also stated that conscience was a social instinct, that the higher animals could and did display a consciousness of guilt and an ability to love.

What he did not say, of course, was that men were descended from apes, but this was the interpretation of his argument put about by the ignorant, and it followed him for the rest of his life. After his death, when it was agreed that a statue of him should be erected in Shrewsbury, in front of his old school, there was great indignation amongst churchgoers, and for a time the statue had to be watched day and night because there were so many threats to damage it.

Charles Darwin himself ignored the uproar caused by his work, retreating more and more into a semi-invalid routine at Down.

He and Emma had ten children, though not all of them lived to grow up. His family was devoted to him; his own awe of his father was not repeated in that generation. He was a man of moderate wealth, respected by scientists all over the world. But in his old age he was filled with melancholy. He never ceased to be conscious of the fact that he had shaken the foundations of belief, though he described himself as an agnostic, always maintaining that such a meticulously planned world must be ordered by some logical, thinking Power.

He was reticent on the subject of religion, but had a deep affection for all forms of life. He loved flowers, and while walking in his garden would frequently touch them gently, as though they could respond to a caress. He was passionately devoted to dogs, and his constant companion, Polly, a rough-haired terrier, survived him by only a few days.

Darwin's last book, published in 1881, was the result of his research on earthworms and their effect upon the soil. His attention had first been drawn to this subject in his Shrewsbury days, when a field to the north of the town was ploughed for the first time and a number of broken weapons—swords, daggers and arrowheads—were found at the bottom of the furrows. These were relics of the Battle of Shrewsbury, left on the ground after the fighting in 1403. Through the ensuing centuries they had been buried under a layer of vegetable mould about nine inches in depth, which had passed through the bodies of innumerable earthworms.

In 1841, as an experiment, Darwin scattered a layer of chalk over part of a field near Down House; by 1871, a line of white nodules could be traced several inches below the surface. He asked a Shrewsbury friend to measure for him the depth of vegetable mould covering the ruins of the Roman city of Uriconium; it varied from nine inches to forty, all deposited by earthworms which had

Statue of Charles Darwin, at the Main Entrance to the Old School, Shrewsbury.

lived above the site for hundreds of years. No wonder he affectionately nicknamed the earthworm "Nature's ploughman".

At the time when his study of *The Foundation of Vegetable Mould Through the Action of Worms* was published, Darwin was old and frail, and realised that he had little time left.

"I have worked as hard and as well as I could", he remarked once, "and no man can do more than this".

On April 19th, 1882, he died quietly at Down after a heart attack. The Church had revised its way of thinking, and the "atheist and blasphemer" was buried in Westminster Abbey, near to that other great scientist, Isaac Newton. He had radically changed the whole science of Biology, and the pattern of his life-work was summed up in his autobiography.

"From my early youth", he wrote, "I have had the strongest desire to understand, or to explain, whatever I observed—that is, to group all facts under some general laws".

Truly an apt promise for the first of modern naturalists.

73

Eglantyne Jebb 1876–1928

Eglantyne Jebb.

The Lyth, Ellesmere, has for generations been occupied by members of the Jebb family. It is a house which gives the visitor an impression of continuity; once inside, one feels that the hall and the large rooms can have changed little since the end of the nineteenth century. The comfortable, well-worn furniture has a place of its own; the walls are hung with portraits of Jebb ancestors, among them sepia photographs of a family of six children. These were the children of Arthur and Eglantyne Jebb, owners of the Lyth at the end of Queen Victoria's reign. Their fourth child, another Eglantyne, was destined to travel, both in body and in spirit. She championed the cause of the helpless, whatever their race, colour or creed, and became the founder of the international movement known as the Save the Children Fund.

Eglantyne's own childhood was as happy and secure as any could wish. Her parents were very conscious of their duty to those less fortunately placed than themselves. The Jebb children absorbed a sense of community service which they looked upon as a natural part of life.

They were a very united family, and the daughters in particular used to say, in all seriousness, that they were doubly fortunate in that they had two mothers. Their "second mother" was their father's unmarried sister, known in the family as "Aunt Bun", who lived all her life at the Lyth or in a converted cottage on the estate, and took an equal share with Mrs. Jebb in running the house and bringing up the children.

A passionate believer in higher education, she was determined that her nieces should have the benefit of a University course. She had a far more forceful personality than her sister-in-law, and all her nephews and nieces adored her, though she never attempted in any way to take their mother's place.

Among the children, the young Eglantyne was a natural leader. At eleven years of age she was a tomboy, organising her brothers and sisters into armies which fought out strategically planned campaigns among the outbuildings and the clumps of rhododendrons, or, in winter, defended carefully built snow ramparts against bombardments of snowballs. But she was a studious child also, enjoying lessons with a succession of governesses, and writing down her thoughts, whether in poetry or in prose, with amazing facility. For three years she edited a family journal which she called "The Briarland Recorder". Copies of it can be seen at The Lyth today, in tattered exercise-books, ruled in columns to make it look like a real newspaper. The beautiful copperplate handwriting is still black and bold, and the material excellent of its kind. Eglantyne herself contributed poems and stories. One serial was entitled "The Ellwyes" and recounted the adventures of a family not unlike the Jebbs. Another, "Eva Drachir", is obviously about herself and her own make-believe world. The other children signed their articles with their own names, but Eglantyne used the pseudonym "R. Hare", because of her mop of red-gold curls. She was easily the most striking of the family in appearance, with long, thick hair, blue eyes, and a creamy skin. Her parents probably expected that she would marry young; Aunt Bun had other ideas.

There had been friction, well-concealed, between Bun and Arthur Jebb on the subject of his daughters' education. She constantly

The Lyth, Ellesmere.

advocated the necessity of a degree course for any girl in a position to benefit from it, he contemptuously observed that he did not want any "blue-stocking" daughters. But in 1894 he died, and the following year, Eglantyne went up to Oxford, to read History. She became a student at Lady Margaret Hall, where her fees were paid by Aunt Bun.

At first she was shy and miserably homesick, but in a very short time she became involved in her work and joined many of the student societies. Because she had beauty and charm in addition to her intelligence, she was very popular, and enjoyed every moment of her three years at Oxford. At the end of her third year, she met the young widow of Arnold Toynbee, founder of the University Settlement in the East End of London, and from this friendship developed her sense of purpose.

Eglantyne Jebb had been brought up in an atmosphere of service to those less fortunate than herself, but somehow she had been aware of something in the relationship which seemed to her to be wrong. Now, taken by Mrs. Toynbee to see for herself the slum conditions in which girls of her own age had been brought up in the East End, she suddenly knew what it was that struck her as unsatisfactory about the philanthropic atmosphere of her home. Always, there were two kinds of people, those who gave and those who received. There was a barrier between them, which she felt ought not to be there, and this barrier was the result of both social position and educational opportunity. She decided that, once she had obtained her degree, she must do something to remove it.

Education, Eglantyne felt, was the key to the problem. Aware of how her own horizons had been widened by her three years at Oxford, she felt that if the minds of socially underprivileged girls could be similarly broadened, the result would be a spirit of independence and equality. She had been inside one of the National Schools in London's

dockland—a dreary, brick building with narrow windows, where the children were crowded sixty to a class, where books and paper were rare luxuries and the lessons consisted of monotonous learning by rote. Encouraged by Mrs. Toynbee and Aunt Bun, but against the wishes of her mother, she became a student at Stockwell Teacher Training College, with the laudable aim of sharing her own educational advantages with others.

Here she met students of a very different type from those who had been her companions at Lady Margaret Hall. They were mostly girls from suburban families, the daughters of trades-people and schoolteachers, clever, but without the breadth of her own leisurely education. Living conditions at the college, too, were far inferior to those to which she had been accustomed, but Eglantyne accepted them without complaint. She was interested in "all sorts and conditions of men"—and women; soon her fellow-students, at first very much on the defensive with her because it was virtually unheard-of for a graduate to embark upon a career as an Elementary School Teacher, were won over by her genuine charm and eagerness to succeed. From her first school practice, however, it was obvious that she was not destined to become a successful teacher—at least, not in conditions prevailing in the schools of that era. Large classes terrified her, and she was quite incapable of maintaining the rigid discipline demanded by head-teachers and Board of Education Inspectors. Advised by her Principal to give up, she insisted on completing the course, but despite her academic brilliance she left Stockwell with a very poor teaching certificate.

As a result, she did not find it easy to obtain a post. The difficult London schools rejected her, and her dream of broadening the vision of the slum child had to be abandoned. In 1899, she took up an appointment at St. Peter's Church School, Marlborough. Here the children were poor enough, living in overcrowded and insanitary cottages. Illness and absences were frequent, and although her pupils as individuals grew very fond of her the necessity for maintaining rigid discipline in a large class was a thing quite beyond her powers.

The two years she spent at Marlborough were two of the unhappiest in Eglantyne's life. She felt a failure because of her total inability to fit into the pattern demanded by her school. Had she but known it, it was the system, not herself, that was at fault. She was a teacher in advance of her time, longing to bring the real world into the dreary routine of the classroom, and to offer her pupils sympathetic understanding. She wanted to make her lessons joyous and exciting periods of discovery, but when children are happy and excited they tend to become vocal, if not vociferous, and a noisy class was considered to be the sign of an incompetent teacher. Just before she gave up teaching in 1901, she wrote in her diary:

I am not interested in the subjects I teach, and so I never could bring myself to care whether the children knew them or not—apart from its being my duty to make them know. However much I tried, I could only keep discipline by nag, nag, nagging. I have never felt I benefited the children at all.

Early in 1901, Eglantyne became ill. At first her family thought her illness was due to physical strain, but later she was found to be suffering from an enlarged thyroid gland, a condition which, together with its consequent over-stimulation of the nervous system, was to trouble her for the rest of her life. She became thin and pale, and her abundant vitality deserted her. Her mother, who had left The Lyth and taken a house at Cambridge, insisted that Eglantyne went to live with her.

In the leisurely atmosphere of Cambridge, Eglantyne's strength gradually returned. She spent a great deal of time considering religion; torn between her mother's conventional piety, her own studies of Eastern mysticism and the hearty scepticism of Aunt Bun—to whom she wrote frequently—she saw herself as one who had no anchor. Gradually, she came to an idea of the universal nature of Christ, a conception that all forms of life were part of the Divinity, and, therefore, sacred. But this belief, though it satisfied her, did not occupy her; she was essentially one of those who must be up and doing. She joined the Cambridge Charity Organisation Society, under whose aegis she published a composite report on poverty in Cambridge, entitled *Cambridge:—a Social Study*. This book, which appeared in 1906, put forward many ideas which we now take for granted. Practical suggestions were made; voluntary workers should collect and invest money to provide pensions for the old (in 1906, there was no national pension scheme). Such voluntary workers should also organise thrift clubs, help crippled children by taking them out, encourage social activities among young people, and take an active part in school management.

That same year, 1906, Eglantyne became interested in politics, supporting the Liberal Party's programme of social reform. She was one of many women mildly committed to the Suffrage movement, but never became so greatly involved as did her younger sister, Dorothy Buxton. Then, in 1907, her mother had a serious illness and Eglantyne left her work at Cambridge to travel with her to Switzerland. They returned to England just before the outbreak of the first Balkan War.

After five hundred years of Turkish domination, the Balkan peoples had made a successful bid for liberation. They were, however, too bitterly divided racially to unite as one country, and for the first time Europe was confronted with a refugee problem of the type which has sadly become only too familiar.

Charles Buxton, the husband of Eglantyne Jebb's sister Dorothy, was a philanthropist who had taken up the problem of these refugees in a practical way. He had organised a Macedonian Relief Fund, which had managed to collect a considerable sum of money. The difficulty, however, was to ensure that this money went to the people who were intended to benefit from it. It was of no use to rely on the incompetent methods of the embryo governments of the Balkan states; what was needed was someone who would take the money out to Macedonia, assess the needs of the various peoples, distribute funds and supplies, and return with a coherent report on what was actually taking place. Charles Buxton would never have entertained the idea of delegating this task to his sister-in-law if it had not been for his wife. But Dorothy knew that, beneath Eglantyne's idealism, lay a sound foundation of common sense. She also knew that her sister, having once undertaken a responsibility, would see it through to the end.

So, in 1913, Eglantyne Jebb went out to the Balkans. Her expedition was comparable to a modern exploration of the upper reaches of the Congo or the Amazon, and, apart from the advice of the British Consul at Monastir and the company of a reliable Serbian interpreter whom he recommended, she was alone. She found the countryside wild and its inhabitants pitifully poor. The only roads were those made by the Romans, and the peasants farmed their land by methods which Europe had discarded with the feudal system. As for the refugees, it was virtually impossible for any Western European to disentangle the problems of their racial hatreds; some were Turkish, some Slav. There were Moslems of many races who were now hounded from their homes by Coptic Christians. She saw Kazan, a Moslem village which the Christians destroyed; she saw in Skoplje Moslem houses razed to the ground. The British Consul at Monastir took her to a camp of about 11,000

Eglantyne Jebb as a student.

refugees of various races and religons. He told her that many were dying daily of typhoid, malnutrition or influenza. She learned that two English pence would maintain a man for a day. But she found the Balkan peoples honest and courteous. It was known that she carried on her person money which, to them, represented untold wealth, yet she was never attacked, she never felt afraid, and no-one ever attempted to interfere with her distribution of the dole collected by her English friends. She heard the bells of the Coptic churches ring for the first time after five hundred years of silence under Turkish rule, and when, her mission accomplished, she returned to England, the people of the Balkans had become to her an important focal point. Constantly she recalled the privations of the refugees at Monastir, and especially the children, bewildered, cowed and hungry.

When war broke out in 1914, Eglantyne was ill. Her Balkan expedition had resulted in intense fatigue which eventually led to an operation for goitre. At heart a pacifist, she did her best to hold aloof from the war-fever which gripped the country. But in 1917 Dorothy Buxton drew her into the activities of the *Cambridge Magazine*.

This was the innocuous title of an international newspaper designed to bring home to thinking people the miseries brought by total war to the civilian population of every country. Charles and Dorothy Buxton were members of the Society of Friends, or Quakers, and there were many who frankly despised their open pacifism. England was at war, and one of the chief weapons of that war was the blockade of European ports by the Allied navies. This blockade was intended to make the import of weapons impossible; it was so successful that it was impossible for continental countries to import anything—and that included food. By the Autumn of 1917, civilians all over Europe were starving to death.

Charles Buxton obtained permission to import, through neutral Sweden, newspapers from many European countries, which were translated by Dorothy, Eglantyne, and a small staff of Cambridge graduates. The *Cambridge Magazine* did not publish any military information; its aim was to make its readers aware of social conditions. In its columns appeared reports of Finnish peasants who had no food other than bark and lichen, of Rumanians dying of cold because they had no fuel, of the infant mortality rate in Germany, Austria and Poland, where women were unable to feed their babies because they themselves were subsisting on a diet of cabbage leaves and turnips. The *Cambridge Magazine* did not make popular reading, but the consciences of an intelligent minority were stirred into an uneasy awareness of the sufferings which resulted from the Allied blockade.

In 1918, the war came to an end with the signature of the Armistice. An Armistice, however, was no Peace Treaty; the fighting was over, but the Blockade of enemy countries continued. In fairness, one must endeavour to reconstruct the emotions of English people after four years of ruthless warfare. In addition to their anxiety, civilians had endured privations on a hitherto unprecedented scale. What people did not realise was that, in comparison to the sufferings of the victors, those of the vanquished were indescribable. Eglantyne Jebb, who had never forgotten the refugee children at Monastir, was one of the few people who could have some conception of the grim aftermath of war. Remembering with a feeling akin to remorse their own secure childhood at the Lyth, she and Dorothy Buxton inaugurated the Fight the Famine Council, its avowed aim to combat the physical and moral effects of starvation in all parts of Europe. The sisters organised meetings and gave lectures on the subject of the physical and moral effects of starvation in

European countries, appealing particularly on behalf of children, innocent victims who bore no responsibility for the war.

As a result of this activity, a special sub-committee of the Fight the Famine Council was formed, with the aim of relieving the suffering of children of all nations. Its international concept did not make for popularity, and many of Eglantyne's and Dorothy's friends advised them against holding a mass meeting on May 19th, 1919, in the Albert Hall, for the purpose of launching the "Save the Children Fund". People would give, they said, to help starving Belgian children; no-one would contribute money or goods to feed Germans or Austrians.

"They are children", was Eglantyne's reply. "How can children be anybody's enemies?"

Three days before the meeting, Eglantyne was arrested on a charge of distributing subversive literature, and fined £5. Knowing that people found it comfortable to believe that reports of the famine were exaggerated, she had printed a large number of leaflets bearing a photograph of an emaciated Viennese baby, with a blunt announcement that there were millions of children, all over Europe, being starved "in the name of Britain".

"What does Britain stand for"? demanded her headline. "Shall this go on?"

Her arrest certainly gave some publicity to the projected appeal. In a letter to her mother on the day of her appearance at Bow Street, Eglantyne wrote:

I asked the man who prosecuted me for a subscription. He intimated he couldn't give me one while the case was pending, but begged me to remind him of it later on.

The police inspectors had tea with me. I think the magistrates were also somewhat sympathetic with my misguided zeal.

The sum of money raised at the Albert Hall meeting exceeded all expectations; the Miners' Trade Union alone collected a donation of £10,000. The Save the Children Fund was now an established body, with Eglantyne Jebb as its secretary. Its first funds were quickly spent on clothing, medical supplies and bedding for orphanages, and the cardinal point of its purpose was that all children, of whatever race, had an equal claim for relief.

Such a vast aim demanded vast resources, and Eglantyne's next move was to appeal through the Churches. She obtained an audience with the Pope, Benedict XV, who was impressed by her sincerity. He urged Catholic congregations all over the world to make special collections for the Save the Children Fund on Holy Innocents' Day, 1919. Other churches followed suit, and an enormous sum was subscribed, which was allocated to providing for the needs of children in all parts of Europe who were suffering as a result of the war.

By this time, National Child Relief Societies were being formed in many countries, but Eglantyne's ideal was a society truly international in its work and constitution. In January, 1920, she went to Geneva, where the infant League of Nations was formulating its aims. Here, in the hall where the International Red Cross had been formed, she addressed the first meeting of the International Save The Children Fund Union, in which all nations and religions were to be involved in work for children's welfare. "A child is a child," she said, "whether red or white, brown or black."

The International nature of the Save the Children Fund attracted some hostility. Socialists objected to the fact that the children of Russian emigrés were given milk provided by the Fund; central European aristocrats resented the dispatch of an International Unit to feed the hungry children of Soviet Russia during the famine of 1921. Many English people observed that there was hunger at home during the post-war depression, and a school for delicate children was established from the Save the Children Fund resources, in acknowledgement of the justice of this complaint. But the cause of the child became an internationally accepted priority. The Declaration of the Rights of the Child, drawn up by Eglantyne Jebb, was endorsed by the League of Nations at its Fifth Assembly. In brief, it stated the right of the child to have protection in time of war, and to grow up in an environment conducive to physical, moral and spiritual development. In times of famine and distress, the children should be the first to receive aid; all children should be trained to earn a livelihood, none should be exploited. But—and here, surely, one detects an echo of her own upbringing—the child must be brought up in the consciousness that its talents must be devoted to the service of its fellow men. This Declaration, which has always formed the basis of the work of the Save the Children Fund, was in 1948 adopted, with only very minor additional clauses, by the United Nations.

During the early 1920's, Eglantyne Jebb travelled widely for the Save the Children Fund. She sponsored a travelling exhibition of the art of Viennese children who were the pupils of Professor Cizek, and opened hospitals for sick children in Hungary. In 1926 she re-visited the Balkans, where in Bulgaria two children's villages had been built, in which war orphans lived as a community, learning agriculture in order to become self-supporting. One of these villages was given her name—Xheba, the nearest the Bulgars could get to the English Jebb.

Eglantyne's health, however, deteriorated. The restless energy which was a by-product of her diseased thyroid gland weakened her heart and wore her out. In 1928, between July and September, she underwent in a Geneva clinic three operations for her goitre. At first, these appeared to have been successful, and in December she left hospital to convalesce at Sierre, on the slopes of Mont Pilatus. Here, on December 17th, she suffered a sudden heart-attack, collapsed and died, at the age of 52.

She was buried at St. George's Cemetery, Geneva, and at first it was feared that the International Save the Children Fund, lacking her driving force, might finish. But it was firmly established, and wherever children were in need, there the Fund's Relief Units travelled, taking food, medical supplies and the means to provide education. Even Hitler's brutal campaigns against Jewish, Czech, Polish and Russian children could not obliterate the work of the Fund, which in 1969 celebrated its fiftieth anniversary. Mercifully, Eglantyne did not see the refugee children of Korea, Biafra and Vietnam, but the work done to rehabilitate them would have given her cause to rejoice. The resilience of children in adversity was the mainspring of her faith in humanity. In her preface to *Save the Child*, she comments on the carelessness with which mankind begets its children. Yet, she concludes, every generation of children born is a promise to humanity that it has another opportunity to re-create its ruined world.

Walford Davies 1869–1941

Sir Walford Davies

In the middle of the nineteenth century the Choir-master of Oswestry Congregational Church, locally known as Christ Church, was John Whitridge Davies. The Davies family had long been connected with Christ Church; John Davies' grandfather had been its Minister, his brother was its organist. John Davies was prominent in the musical life of the town; in addition to his work at the church he taught music—he could play the violin and was an accomplished pianist—and in 1850 he founded the Oswestry Choral Society. One of its original members was Susan Gregory, the daughter of a local jeweller. She was a member of the Congregational Church and there she and John Davies were married. They took a house in Willow Street, and had a large family. When her seventh child was expected, Susan Davies longed for a daughter. However, the child born on 6th September, 1869 was another boy. He was given the names Henry Walford (Walford was the maiden name of his grandmother) and his life-story certainly bore out the old superstition that a seventh child is born fortunate and different from all others.

Walford, as he was always called, was as a child very close to his mother and the bond lasted until he went away to school at twelve years of age. From his mother he obtained the profound religious faith which pervaded all his work. From his father he inherited a more practical gift, his musical ability. Not only was John Davies a good choir-master and conductor; he was also a proficient instrumentalist. All of his children were taught to play some instrument. They were also encouraged to teach one another, so that each was able to perform on any of several instruments with reasonable skill. From these early music lessons at home grew Walford's belief that all young people have some talent for music.

It was during these early years in Oswestry that Walford first showed himself capable of improvisation and composition. In common with many other Victorian families, the Davies' possessed a harmonium. Walford taught himself to play this, and was soon improvising happily on various well-known tunes. His uncle taught him to play the organ in church, and when he joined the choir it was obvious that his soprano voice was of rare quality.

Christ Church, Oswestry.

At this time he was attending a private school in Willow Street, not far from his home. His father, however, was convinced that the boy's musical talent was above the ordinary, and he was enough of a musician himself to recognise the beauty of his son's voice. He learned from a friend that there was to be an audition at St. George's Chapel, Windsor, where twelve boys were accepted annually as choristers. He proposed taking Walford to London so that the organist and choir-master, Sir George Elvey, might try his voice. He knew that his son's musical gifts could not be fully developed in a little town on the borders of Wales. To London he and Walford went, and in 1882 the boy obtained a place as a chorister at St. George's Chapel.

At first, his general education, apart from music, was no better than he had received at the Oswestry school, and he found himself in advance of his contemporaries in most subjects. The choristers' routine was a monotonous one, but when Walter Parratt became organist in 1884 the curriculum was widened. He was professor of organ studies at the newly-formed Royal College of Music, and saw clearly that a successful musician must also develop skills in other fields.

Early in 1885, Walford's voice broke, but Dr. Parrat, aware of this pupil's skill as an organist, advised him to stay on at St. George's for a time as his assistant. Walford went home to Oswestry in February and eagerly put the plan before his father. John Davies approved, understanding that it was now impossible to tear him away from the world of church music. But, before the end of Walford's Easter holiday, his father died. The boy was sixteen, and he knew that if any future lay before him as a musician, he must now fend for himself.

He was fortunate, for two new influences came into his life. On his return to Windsor the Dean, Dr. Davidson, who had heard of his plight, offered him a post as his secretary. Walford was never very methodical about anything except music, but Dr. Davidson bore with him, for he knew that it was essential for Walford to complete his education at the choir school.

The other new friends came from nearer home. John Davies had a cousin, Edward Woodall, who was the owner of the local newspaper, the *Oswestry Advertizer*. "Uncle Edward", as he was known to the younger members of the Davies family, had friends in London, a Mr. and Mrs. Matheson, who lived at Hampstead. Prompted by Mr. Woodall, they invited Walford to visit them. Mrs. Matheson felt sorry for the thin, gauche boy who had so lately lost his father. She and her husband belonged to a musical circle, and Walford said in later life that it was Mrs. Matheson who taught him to really listen to his own playing. In 1890, as a result of her encouragement, he sat for the examination for the degree of Mus. Bac. at Cambridge. He failed, but in that same year he did win a Foundation Scholarship to the newly-formed Royal College of Music. Here he studied Composition; Piano and Violin playing, and gained his Mus. Bac. at the end of his second year.

The advantages to him as a composer were inestimable. He had also the stimulus of books, plays and conversation outside the College sphere, for the Mathesons, had adopted him into their family as another son, though during the holidays he always returned to Oswestry, staying either at Willow Street or with "Uncle" Edward Woodall.

In 1894 his scholarship ended, and he took the post of organist at Christ Church, Hampstead. In addition, he began to compose cantatas and settings for some of the psalms, and that year gave his first public concert of his own works.

The following year he was appointed to the staff of the Royal College of Music as teacher of counterpoint. He was a gifted teacher, capable of making any part of his subject interesting to his pupils. As he was not himself a good examination candidate, he refused to make the examination the sole aim, but he would indicate to his pupils that, first and foremost, any musical course was worth following for its own sake.

In 1896, he published his setting for *Weep Ye No More Sad Fountains*; the same year he went to Vienna, armed with a letter of introduction to Brahms. His interview with the composer was short, though on the whole satisfactory. Brahms looked through several of his compositions and spoke approvingly of some of them.

Mrs Matheson advised Walford to apply for the post of organist of the Temple Church, the church of the Benchers of the Inner and Middle Temple. There were almost a hundred candidates, for the post was one of great prestige in the world of music, and from these, three finalists were selected to play the organ and accompany the choir before the appointing committee. Walford was the successful one. He learned afterwards that the choir boys, with whom he soon became very popular, had played a part in his election. Before the decision was finally made, they had been asked which organist's accompaniment they most enjoyed singing to, and they replied in unison "Dr. Davies'". He took up his new appointment in February 1898, and held it, with a break for war service in 1916–1918, until 1919.

For ten months of every year Walford was occupied with services at the Temple, but the church was closed during August and September, so he had time for composition. He dealt with his choirboys in much the same way as his father had dealt with his family at home, encouraging them to teach one another. When they were learning a difficult piece, any boy who sang the troublesome part correctly was told to sing it for the others, until they had learned it from him. He was never short of soloists, for every chorister had to take a solo part in his turn. He addressed all the boys by nicknames, and insisted that they received a good general education. One of the reforms initiated by Walford was their transfer to the City of London School, where they would mix with boys who had interests outside the field of music. The choristers' education was financed by the barristers, which was a great inducement to parents to send their sons to the Temple. Among his pupils were Leopold Stokowski, the conductor, and the composer, Rutland Boughton.

During the first ten years of this century Walford Davies became well-known in the world of music. Sir Edward Elgar became interested in his work and persuaded the Worcester Festival Committee to invite him to compose a work to be performed at the Three Choirs Festival in 1902. The result was "The Temple", a choral setting for the Biblical verses describing Solomon's building. In 1904 the Leeds Festival Choir performed his cantata *Everyman*. This had a great success, and was followed by a performance in London, by the Queen's Hall Orchestra, of some of his suites. In 1908, the tercentenary of Milton's birth, he was asked to take charge of the music for a special service held in Bow Church in honour of the occasion. Here his best-known composition, *Solemn Melody*, was heard for the first time.

When war broke out in 1914 Walford was 45, over military age. He had his work at the Temple and occasionally taught at the Royal College of Music, but he was very anxious to do something to help the war effort, and in 1916 managed to get himself sent to France to help entertain the troops. He displayed an amazing talent for making anybody and everybody interested in music. With only his voice and an out-of-tune piano at a base camp to help him, he managed to get the soldiers singing, not only war songs but folk songs, part songs and the kind of hymns he taught his Temple choir. In 1918

the Royal Air Force was formed and Walford was appointed its first Director of Music. He composed the R.A.F. official March Past, and in 1919, at a Memorial Service held in Westminster Abbey for members of the R.A.F., his *Memorial Melody* for strings, drums and organ was performed.

Walford Davies left the Temple in 1919, to become the first Director of Music for the University of Wales. Immediately he found himself involved in the musical life of the Principality. His students, finding him so readily accessible, would tell him of eisteddfau and festivals in their own home valleys and churches, and sometimes requested him to attend one to listen, to criticise, to adjudicate. He gave to each of the amateur singers or instrumentalists with whom he came into contact the same careful attention that he had bestowed upon his choristers at the Temple; he never hurried, he was always ready to offer advice and encouragement, always approachable. These qualities soon became known, and he was in such great demand that, in addition to his work at Aberystwyth, he was travelling to schools, churches and village halls all over North Wales.

There was one thing which troubled Walford about the attitude of the Welsh towards music—they were imbued with a competitive spirit. He believed firmly that, in order for its joys to be known to the full, music-making should be a shared experience. All these contests, he felt, were depriving people of a great deal of pleasure. Just as in his old days at the Royal College of Music he had refused to consider the examination to be the main end of the course, so he now set out to teach the people of Wales that the aim of music-making was to give pleasure to the performers and audience alike.

In this cause he soon enlisted two active and wealthy helpers. The Misses Gwendolen and Margaret Davies of Gregynog Hall, near

Newtown, Montgomeryshire, sisters of the first Lord Davies, were music lovers and from their first meeting with Walford, supported all his aims. Gregynog was already used for small, private concerts; now they offered it for music-making on a grand scale. It became the headquarters of the Welsh National Council of Music, the object of which was to bring good music within the reach of any and every person. The Hall was thrown open for concerts, festivals and Summer Schools, and at all of these Walford was the presiding genius.

He did more than anyone else to generate the Welsh passion for music. Sometimes, he found it uphill work, for his kind of music was not the music of nationalism, and that, often, was what an Eisteddfod audience had assembled to hear. On one occasion, his choir steadily sang through Bach's St. Matthew Passion, in spite of the opposition of a section of their listeners who made their resentment felt by a tuneful rendering of *Land of my Fathers* in Welsh. On the whole, however, his innovations were well-received. He still found time for composition; in 1920 his *Fantasy* was performed at the Three Choirs Festival, and his old friend Sir Edward Elgar was there to hear it.

The following year, Walford was saddened by the death of his 'adopted' mother, Mrs. Matheson. Suddenly, in the midst of people and work, he found himself lonely. His own mother had died years before, his brothers and one of his sisters were married and with growing families; he alone seemed rootless and insecure. His friends at Aberystwyth, sensing his need for a background, took a house for him, 'Rhydyfyrian', on the outskirts of the town, where he spent five happy years.

In 1922 the Welsh Symphony Orchestra was formed under his direction. Its headquarters were the concert hall at Gregynog, but it played at National Eisted-

fodau, Festivals, and at the Three Valleys Festival, which he instituted as a similar organisation to the Three Choirs Festival. In 1928 the Orchestra performed Elgar's Oratorio *The Apostles* at the Harlech Festival and the composer himself was their guest conductor. A knighthood was conferred upon Walford in 1922, in recognition of his work at the Temple and his services to Welsh music.

In 1924 came the Empire Exhibition at Wembley. Here, in a gigantic arena, were exhibited the crafts, industries and products of all parts of the British Empire. Each country was allocated a week in which to display its national songs, dances and drama, and during Welsh Week, Sir Walford Davies took to London the Welsh Symphony Orchestra, together with an All-Welsh choir of 4,000 voices, for by this time South Wales, too, had been drawn into his musical net.

Walford was fifty-five years old when he married. His bride, Margaret Evans, shared her husband's love for music. They settled very happily at "Rhydyfyrian", and Margaret relieved him of a great deal of the secretarial work necessitated by his many activities.

During the first few years of the 1920's, broadcasting became a part of national life. In 1924, Walford was invited to attend an advisory committee on music, set up by the B.B.C. at its new headquarters at Savoy Hill. He already had some sense of the power of "music by machine", for he was a member of the Educational Department of His Master's Voice Gramophone Company, and was a great advocate of the use of records as a teaching aid, so that recordings of orchestras and singers could be used in the classroom, as a supplement to the established routine of singing to the piano. This innovation was not always successful; in his eagerness to give children the opportunity to hear great performers, he did not realise that all teachers of music did not possess his own knack of arousing interest.

Broadcasting, however, gave him an opportunity to do his own teaching. His first broadcast lesson for school children was given from Savoy Hill on April 4th, 1924. He talked to his unseen audience, played excerpts from well-known scores, and brought some of the Temple choristers to the studio to sing.

His technique was successful, and his manner rapidly established him as a radio personality. He had an ideal voice for broadcasting, easily identifiable, and he talked to the children as though he were in their classroom beside them. He involved the teachers, and before long was producing pamphlets and song-books, which were published by the B.B.C., to supplement his lessons. His broadcasts to schools went on the air at regular intervals for the next ten years, during which period he gave over 400 lessons, produced eighty pamphlets and directed at least seventy children's concerts in the studio.

In 1926 he embarked upon a similar series for adults, *Music and the Ordinary Listener*, in which he set out to teach the ordinary man and woman the fundamentals of musical composition, so that they would be able to listen to a piece of music with greater understanding and, consequently, greater enjoyment. These years between the wars were the high-watermark of broadcasting, and Sir Walford Davies was one of those who became an established radio personality because of his voice, his turn of phrase—"Good evening, listeners all" was his invariable opening—and his ability to project his own deep involvement with his subject over the microphone. *Music and the Ordinary Listener* was followed by *Keyboard Talks* and *Melodies of Christendom*. How much of his lessons the "ordinary listener" understood is a debatable point, but people with no musical background listened to him for the sheer enjoyment of hearing him play and talk. Sir Walford Davies was one of those

who helped to make broadcasting a national institution.

In 1929 he resigned from the staff of Aberystwyth University; he was 57, and his heart was not as strong as it had been. However, he still continued broadcasting and working for the Welsh Council of Music. The following year he was appointed organist and choirmaster of St. George's Chapel, Windsor. One of his immediate duties there was to supervise the building of a new organ, and on the occasion of its first use in public he accompanied the united choirs of all the Royal Chapels as they sang in unison to his playing.

One of his many offices was that of honorary Director of Music to the Boy Scout movement, and in the summer of 1929 scouts from all over the world made camp in Arrow Park, Birkenhead, where a Grand Jamboree was held. It was an exceptionally wet summer, but the programme was carried through, and one of the events was an afternoon of community singing by the massed Scouts, conducted by Sir Walford Davies. Rain descended ceaselessly, and the boys came from many nations and spoke many languages; to achieve enjoyable community singing seemed an impossibility. Sir Walford, however, was equal to the occasion. Wearing white flannels so that he could be seen, and gum-boots because of the state of the ground, he mounted his rostrum and within fifteen minutes had all the boys singing tunefully and in unison, despite the steady downpour.

When Sir Edward Elgar died in 1934, Sir Walford Davies was appointed his successor as Master of the King's Musick. One of his first duties was to superintend the musical arrangements for King George V's Silver Jubilee in 1935. He proposed a national concert of British music, to be given in the Albert Hall. He conducted a huge orchestra, and choirs came from England, Scotland, Ireland and Wales to sing their own national songs.

And, in January, 1936, when George V died, it was Sir Walford Davies who selected the music that was played at the various services broadcast while the King lay dying.

He played a major part in organizing the music used at the coronation of George VI and arranged another concert of national music. He was also the promoter of a special Coronation Concert for children which was attended by the Queen and her two daughters. For this occasion he wrote a suite of tunes to which he gave the title *Big Ben Looks On*, and arranged a simple piano score for these, which he presented to the young princesses so that they would be able to play them for themselves. It was the first opportunity he had had for composition since leaving Aberystwyth.

Sir Walford Davies gave new life to the old Office of Master of the King's Musick, so that it became something really vital in the existence of the nation. One of the things which gave him great pleasure was that, soon after his appointment to the Office was announced, the people of his birthplace invited him back to Oswestry, to be made an honorary freeman of the town.

When war broke out in 1939, Sir Walford Davies was seventy years of age. He had given up the choir of St. George's and, though still working for the B.B.C., he was living with Lady Davies in semi-retirement at Cookham. However, the outbreak of war brought with it a massive evacuation scheme. Various Government departments left the Capital. The Department for Religious Broadcasting, to which he was attached at the time, removed to Bristol.

Sir Walford and Lady Davies went to Bristol, where they took a flat not far from the Cathedral. Here, Walford resumed his broadcasts to schools, and invited groups of children from various Bristol schools to the studio to provide a genuine class. He felt very strongly that music should play a larger part in the wartime radio programmes. As always,

Sir Walford Davies receiving the Freedom of Oswestry.

he believed that the experience of sharing music together would unite and strengthen the population. From this idea was born, in 1940, the Pilgrim Trust, of which Walford was a founder-member. From the Pilgrim Trust developed C.E.M.A.—the Council for the Encouragement of Music and the Arts—which, during and after the war, financed projects whereby music, drama, poetry, art and dance were taken to the provinces, and ordinary people were themselves encouraged to develop their creative abilities.

The long-expected aerial bombardment began at last, not only on London, but on large provincial cities, among them Bristol. Sir Walford and Lady Davies remained in their flat, however, and he continued with his broadcasts, and even found time for some composition. But, early in March, 1941 he contracted pleurisy. His heart, already weak, could not withstand the illness and on March 11th, he died. His ashes were buried in the Garden of Rest of Bristol Cathedral.

Agnes Hunt 1867–1948

Agnes Hunt.

The Hunts of Baschurch have been part of the life of the village since the time of Edward I. In 1867, at their home, Boreatton Park, Agnes Hunt was born, the sixth of a large family of eleven children. Agnes was a lively, active child. Her mother, a very strong-minded woman, believed that children should be allowed to develop their own initiative. Her daughters as well as her sons were allowed the freedom of the grounds, to climb, to ride, to swim in the brook. Mrs. Hunt made only one stipulation; the girls must be prepared to accept their brothers' standards of behaviour. They must expect no concessions on the grounds of sex.

To Agnes, who had never known anything else, liberty was as natural as life itself. She was included in the boys' games as an equal, she was frequently the organiser of many family escapades, for she had the qualities of a born leader. The physical disability which she first faced when she was nine years old could easily have proved overwhelming. The fact that she not only overcame it, but turned it into an instrument for good, was due partly to her own personality and partly to her mother's.

She developed an abscess on her leg. It was very painful, but at first she did not tell anyone about it. Eventually, however, it became so sore that she fainted. The family doctor diagnosed "a bone tumor" and decreed that she must wear an iron calliper and rest as much as possible. But the abscess was the first manifestation of the osteomyelitis which continued to plague her for the rest of her life.

Mrs. Hunt refused to permit her daughter to indulge in self-pity. The result was to build up in the girl a spirit of independence and self-confidence. She was eternally grateful to her mother for making her realise that a physical handicap need not necessarily mean the end of active, normal life.

When Agnes was twelve years old, her father died. Waiting only to see her eldest son installed as master of the Boreatton estate, Mrs. Hunt decided to visit another son, Tom, who had emigrated to Tasmania. Agnes, in whom she already recognised a spirit which matched her own audacity, was to accompany her.

The journey was, at that time, a great undertaking. The voyage out lasted almost three months and Tom Hunt's ranch was in the Tasmanian outback. There were no near neighbours, and supplies arrived at very irregular intervals. For their food the members of the little community depended on their own ingenuity.

Agnes revelled in the excitement of a pioneer's life. By the time she was fifteen she had learned to shoot, and was able to ride most of Tom's horses. She learned the art of falling soft, so as not to damage her lame leg, and every time she was thrown she doggedly got up, set her lips and re-mounted. She got on well with Tom's employees, too. Agnes' steady refusal to be hampered by her lameness was a quality they admired and understood, especially during the year after Mrs. Hunt returned to England, when the girl remained as Tom's housekeeper. She was twenty when she went back home with Tom, who was leaving Tasmania to be married.

After this adventurous interlude Mrs. Hunt had no intention of settling quietly in Baschurch. She took a house in London and engaged herself in a number of charitable concerns, in visiting and helping and organising. Agnes, with her mother's backing, decided to train as a nurse.

Despite the reforms instituted by Florence Nightingale, nursing was still not considered to be a suitable occupation for a young lady of good family. Agnes was turned down by two London hospitals because she was lame, but eventually she was accepted as a "lady-pupil" at the Royal Alexandra Hospital, Rhyl. A "lady-pupil" was expected to pay fees for her training.

The Royal Alexandra had a large proportion of crippled children amongst its patients, sent there because the sea air was invigorating. The matron advocated "fresh air and happiness" as a major part of their treatment. She was particularly interested in cripples, and for this reason was attracted to Agnes. Agnes, in her turn, always remembered her time at Rhyl as a period of great happiness.

Although the Royal Alexandra received pupils the hospital was not able to issue certificates, so to complete her training Agnes went to the West London Hospital, Hammersmith. Here she found very different conditions, the nurses living in great discomfort, overworked and poorly fed. Like many other probationers, Agnes eventually became ill. For six weeks she was in bed, the victim of utter physical exhaustion, and it was at this time that she resolved that, should she herself ever became a matron, no nurse in her hospital should ever suffer physical deprivation in the course of her work for the sick.

It was not until 1891, when she was twenty-four, that Agnes received her final certificate at the Royal Salop Infirmary. She then returned to Hammersmith in order to train for district nursing, and met another nurse, Emily Goodford, a daughter of the Provost of Eton. The two became lifelong friends, and worked together until Miss Goodford's death in 1920.

Mrs. Hunt had been travelling abroad, visiting various members of her family. In 1900 she returned and announced her intention of making her home with Agnes, now her only unmarried daughter. Agnes firmly pointed out that her life as a district nurse left her very little leisure time in which to act as her mother's companion. Mrs. Hunt replied, with equal firmness, that she did expect companionship, but intended to have a home. Florence House, Baschurch, a large, red-brick house belonging to the Boreatton estate, was empty. Agnes and "Goody" should start a convalescent home there, for patients sent by the Royal Salop Infirmary. No, the Infirmary had not expressed any wish for a convalescent home in the country, but it needed one; she would make all the necessary arrangements.

Such was the power of Mrs. Hunt's personality that, in the summer of 1900, Agnes and "Goody" moved, reluctantly, into Florence House, soon to be known as "The Baschurch Home". They had no idea that they were inaugurating the first open-air orthopædic hospital in the world; they had no idea that they would soon be pioneering an entirely new treatment for orthopædic patients. All they knew was that the house was damp and the drinking-water came from a well under the scullery floor; the garden was wild, the drainage primitive, and the Royal Salop Infirmary considered their offer to nurse convalescent patients to be something of an embarrassment. However, a small committee of local people was convened; the local doctor agreed to act as honorary medical officer, and on October 1st, 1900, the Royal Salop Infirmary was informed that Sister Hunt and Sister Goodford were ready to receive eight child patients in need of country air and good food.

The first children who came to the Baschurch Home were all cripples. At the beginning of the century congenital bone disease was usually incurable; rickets and tubercular infection of the bones were both all too common. The usual fate of a crippled child was to spend all its life lying in a dark, stuffy room. Those who received hospital treatment were seldom permanently cured, although sometimes operations which alleviated their condition were performed. The children sent to Agnes Hunt and Emily Goodford were to have rest and nourishing food in order to build up their strength in preparation for such operations. Very often, after a long stay at Baschurch, the operation was not necessary. Good food and complete freedom to play in the overgrown garden whenever they wished often cured rickets so that the patient, though probably not upright, attained a high degree of mobility. The Royal Salop Infirmary began to take notice of the Baschurch Home; more patients were sent but the accommodation had its limits.

One of the most extraordinary aspects of the history of the world's first open-air orthopædic hospital was the casual way in which important new developments originated. A happy-go-lucky air pervaded the place, but below this was the will-power of Agnes Hunt, who was determined to give these children as much help as her mother had given her.

One of the first discoveries made about Florence House was that its staircase was a death-trap. All the children had difficulty in negotiating its steep, narrow treads, and when a spinal case arrived, who had to be carried, the difficulty was seen to be unsuperable. Agnes was determined that he should not be taken to the upstairs "wards" on a stretcher and left there for the remainder of his stay at the Home.

She remembered her grounding at Rhyl. She had already demonstrated the efficacy of fresh air and good food in the treatment of cripples. If he were kept warm and dry, why should not the child be in the fresh air day and night?

With the help of her groom, who was an old servant of the Hunt family, some wooden sheds were moved from the grounds of Boreatton Park and erected in the garden of Florence House. The sheds were completely

Florence House, Baschurch.

open to the air along one side, and here the less mobile patients were installed. They did not catch pneumonia—indeed, those with chest coughs recovered. Waterproof sheets protected the beds from driving rain and snow, and in winter extra blankets and hot water-bottles were provided. Open-air treatment had come to stay.

In summer, Agnes sent the children into the fields for picnics. Those who were able, walked. Those who could sit in push chairs, a wheel-chair or a bath-chair, were pushed. Those obliged to lie flat were not left behind; for them, Agnes had a well-sprung mattress hoisted onto a dray, where they lay in state while the equipage was drawn through the village by Bobby, the Home's pony. And always she was with them, directing, controlling, but never prohibiting. She knew, from first-hand experience, what it felt like to be a crippled child.

An open-air hospital is more expensive to run than a more orthodox one. Fresh air and activity create healthy appetites; better food is needed, more blankets, more hot water, more warm clothing. The funds of the Baschurch Home were always low, and all kinds of schemes were devised in order to raise money. There was no government grant, and subscribers were asked to give eight shillings a week to maintain a child at the Home. In 1902, with an income of £415, the Home dealt with over one hundred cases. That year, the cripples acted a play in order to raise funds. Every child took part, those unable to walk being pushed about the stage on wooden trolleys concealed under the small actors' flowing robes. Some people had qualms about this—surely such deformities ought not to be made public? But Agnes was firm. The children enjoyed the occasion hugely and took a great pride in their independence. The Baschurch Home play became an annual event.

Agnes, untiring in her activities on behalf of "her" crippled children, forgot that she herself was also a cripple. In 1903 her diseased leg was again troubling her. It eventually became obvious that if she did not have treatment she would soon be unable to walk. Someone recommended Robert Jones, a Liverpool surgeon, so Agnes consulted him; in this way began a friendship which lasted until his death, thirty years later.

Robert Jones performed a successful operation on Agnes Hunt's hip, and before long she was able to walk again, although she always had to use a crutch. He found her personality impressive, and, fascinated by her racy account of the Baschurch Home, asked to come and see it. What he saw delighted him. He had never seen crippled children like these—sunburned, independent, happy and entirely free from self-pity. He told Agnes that, if she could arrange transport, he would examine as many of her children as she could bring to his Liverpool Hospital, and would keep one day each month free for the Baschurch Home patients.

The journey to Liverpool was a formidable obstacle, but the opportunity of treatment by the leading orthopædic surgeon of the day could not be missed. Agnes mobilised the residents of Baschurch, and the Station Officials. Every available conveyance was pressed into service to transport the children to the station, where an extra compartment was attached to the Birkenhead train. They greatly enjoyed crossing the Mersey to Liverpool—several of them were hauled on board the ferry boat on a porter's luggage trolley. On one occasion Agnes was asked by a lady on board the ferry if she were responsible for the children; Agnes replied enthusiastically that she was, whereupon her interlocutor, with an expression of horror, pressed into her hand a tract bearing the heading "The Wages of Sin is Death".

"Not in this case", was the unrepentant reply.

However, the monthly journey to Liverpool was obviously a hazard, and the children who were unable to make it needed Robert Jones' skill even more than those who went. In 1904 he offered his services as honorary orthopædic surgeon, promising to spend one day at Baschurch every month, examine the patients and perform such operations as were necessary. Agnes unhesitatingly accepted his offer. It was

"Goody" who pointed out that there was no operating theatre at Florence House.

Nothing daunted, Agnes set out to provide one. The dining room was stripped of all its furniture except the large table. All the face-cloths available, and several sheets, were boiled in a fish-kettle, and another fish-kettle of boiling water was ready to sterilise the instruments. In these primitive conditions, with the local doctor acting as his anaesthetist and "Goody" and Agnes as theatre sisters, Robert Jones performed his operations. Towards the end of his first visit, at dusk, Mrs. Hunt's newly installed acetyline lamps were lighted. They flared bravely for a minute, then went out; the last operation was finished by candle light. But by now Robert Jones was as enthusiastic as Agnes Hunt about the success of Baschurch Home, and came every month until the outbreak of War in 1914.

He interested other surgeons in the success of the new treatment advocated at Baschurch and brought them to see the results. Children from counties other than Shropshire were sent to Baschurch. He urged Agnes to train pupil-nurses in her methods, and helped her to raise the money needed to convert the Home into a hospital. In 1907 an operating theatre was built—it cost the vast sum of £249, and probably no modern surgeon would deign to set foot in it. By 1908 some wooden cubicles had been erected in the garden as quarters for nurses, and the first trainees arrived. But it was not until 1910, when an X-ray plant was installed and the Home was given official recognition by the Chartered Society of Massage, that Baschurch was able to offer acceptable certificates to orthopædic nurses and physiotherapists.

In order to fulfil its function as an orthopædic hospital, the Baschurch Home had to supply surgical appliances to its patients. They were essential and expensive, and Agnes hit upon the plan of having them made on the premises. Her invaluable groom installed a forge and two more sheds purloined from her brother's estate. The first surgical appliance constructed at Baschurch was made from an iron bed-frame, heated and beaten into shape at the forge. With the addition of canvas and padding, it was completely functional and more were made, under supervision, by the older, mobile patients. The slender resources of the Home were stretched to pay them a small wage for their labour, and experts were introduced to give instruction in the niceties of making crutches and surgical boots. From this nucleus was born the scheme which was eventually to make disabled patients self-supporting.

Early in 1914, the Baschurch Home was asked to act as a rest-centre for the wounded in the event of war. After Mrs. Hunt's death there were some empty rooms at Florence House and Agnes had inherited from her mother Boreatton Farm Cottage, a small farmhouse on the estate. This, she thought, would be a useful place to which patients could be moved if extra accommodation were needed. She and "Goody" agreed that the Home could be used as a rest-centre if necessary; they assumed that, in the highly unlikely circumstance of a battle being fought at Oswestry, the wounded soldiers would be brought to Baschurch for elementary first-aid before being taken to the Royal Salop Infirmary for treatment. However, by 1916, Florence House, the open-air ward and two large tents in the garden were filled with wounded soldiers, and the orthopaedic patients had been removed to Boreatton. Robert Jones' visits had ceased, for he was in the R.A.M.C., but Agnes and "Goody" now had a staff of V.A.D.'s in addition to their pupil-nurses, a clerical staff and a retinue of visiting doctors.

By 1917 the extraordinary results of the open-air treatment given at the Baschurch Home had become a matter of public interest. Shropshire County Council, suddenly proud of the little pioneering centre, undertook to send to the Home all children in its care who suffered from surgical tuberculosis, and in 1918 the Council announced that it accepted responsibility for crippled children in the County until they became fourteen years of age. It was the first public body in the world to take such a step.

There were in 1918 a number of patients, who had been discharged from the Home, but required after-care. Those who were mobile came at intervals to centres in some of the towns, but some needed home visits, and many lived in remote areas right away from any station. The first After-Care Sister made her visits on a motor-bike. She had learned how to start the machine, but did not know how to stop it; it was little short of a miracle that she was not herself a patient before the end of her first week's pilgrimage. However, by the end of the year she was making weekly visits to thirteen centres in various parts of Shropshire. At the same time the withdrawal of the wounded soldiers from Florence House began.

In 1919, the British Red Cross Society distributed its surplus funds. Baschurch Home received a donation of £25,000 towards the cost of building a new, up-to-date hospital. The Shropshire War Memorial contributed £9,000 and Agnes, on behalf of the Committee, selected a suitable site. Eventually the Military Hospital at Park Hall, Gobowen, two miles from Oswestry, was purchased. The long wards were made open on one side; the isolation block was converted for use as a laundry and a forge; a workshop and a garage for the Ambulance were erected. In February, 1921, the Shropshire Orthopædic Hospital was ready for occupation. The patients left Baschurch, and Florence House once more became a dwelling house.

Emily Goodford did not move to Park Hall. She died in 1920 after a short illness,

Agnes Hunt and Sir Robert Jones.

leaving Agnes to organise the new hospital alone. One of her first acts was to supervise the construction in its grounds of a small memorial chapel to her friend. They had worked together for thirty years, and it seemed to Agnes that without "Goody" some of the zest had gone from her lifework.

Robert Jones was soon at the new hospital, demobilised and with a knighthood. Student-nurses were eager to train there, and Agnes initiated one of the earliest provincial schools of Physiotherapy. Before long there were so many patients (other counties were by now sending their crippled children to Shropshire for treatment) that a school had to be started in the wards. Physically disabled adults were taught to work and employed in the hospital workshops.

In 1924, after another operation on her hip, Agnes relinquished the active supervision of the hospital and retired to Baschurch Farm Cottage. She had now been created a Dame of the British Empire, and although no longer nursing she busied herself with fund-raising projects. At least once a week she toured the hospital, a familiar figure in her blue uniform, limping about the wards on her crutch. In 1927 the hospital bought a piece of land known as the Derwen, on which bungalows and workshops were erected. Here, cripples were able to live and earn, free from the routine imposed of necessity by any institution. The Derwen Cripples' Training College had come into being, the first settlement of its kind.

After the death in 1933 of Sir Robert Jones, the name of the hospital was changed to "The Robert Jones and Agnes Hunt Orthopædic Hospital". Dame Agnes had watched its development from the primitive sheds in the garden of Florence House to a flourishing open-air hospital. But she was not yet satisfied with the work done at the Derwen. The cripples trained there were all employed by the Hospital. She felt that there ought to be opportunities for some, at least, to do work in other fields. She began a campaign with this end in view, but in the years between the wars it was difficult for a fit man to find employment. The outside world was not interested in the rehabilitation of the physically handicapped.

Just before the outbreak of the Second World War, Dame Agnes went herself to live in one of the bungalows at the Derwen. Once more she saw soldiers installed in some of the wards of the Hospital, although the disruption of the patients' routine was much less than it had been twenty-three years earlier. Whenever she was fit enough to do so, she inspected the wards, talking to the patients, alert, brisk and refusing to be incapacitated by her lameness. But by the end of the War her visits had become infrequent, until her active participation in the life of the Hospital almost ceased.

One bitter night in January, 1948, a fire broke out in the Physiotherapy Department. It raged for three hours, destroying a large section of the Hospital, though fortunately all the patients were evacuated before it reached the wards, and no-one was hurt.

Rebuilding began at once and the work proceeded rapidly. Under the auspices of the new National Health Service a complex of buildings was erected. The Robert Jones and Agnes Hunt Hospital remains one of the most forward-looking establishments of its kind. There are now fewer crippled children, for the diseases caused by malnutrition are seldom seen and innoculation has virtually eradicated poliomyelitis and tuberculosis. The majority of the patients are accident victims; many are completely cured, but rehabilitation is a major feature of the Hospital's work. In 1974, four of the gold medals awarded at the British Commonwealth Paraplegic Games went to patients and ex-patients. This would have delighted Dame Agnes Hunt, and a step taken in the same year by the Shropshire Education Authority marks the culmination of her work. Under their auspices, new training centres have been opened at the Derwen, where both boys and girls who are crippled are taught skills which will fit them for employment outside the Hospital. In this way it is hoped that her aim, which was always to make the cripple into a self-supporting, acceptable member of the community, will finally be achieved.

But Dame Agnes did not live to see the completion of this Hospital. She died in July, 1948, and her ashes were buried in the village churchyard at Baschurch. In the church, a memorial plaque bears her name and the words:

Reared in suffering, thou shalt know
How to solace others' woe.
The reward of pain doth lie,
In the gift of sympathy.